LITTLE BOOK OF
BADMINTON

LITTLE BOOK OF
BADMINTON

First published in the UK in 2013

© G2 Entertainment Limited 2013

www.G2ent.co.uk

Printed and bound in China

ISBN 978-1-782811-98-5

The views in this book are those of the author but they are general views only and readers are urged to consult the relevant and qualified specialist for individual advice in particular situations.

G2 Entertainment Limited hereby exclude all liability to the extent permitted by law of any errors or omissions in this book and for any loss, damage or expense (whether direct or indirect) suffered by a third party relying on any information contained in this book.

Contents

Introduction

Badminton is famous for two things: the shuttlecock game first played in the hall of the house and the world famous Horse Trials. *Little Book of Badminton* is about the latter. Badminton is one of the great sporting events in Britain, and draws crowds of up to 150,000 over the four days of competition in early May each year. It is situated at the Duke of Beaufort's estate on the Gloucestershire and Wiltshire borders and has been run since 1949. There have been just one or two cancellations in that time, when either the weather or foot and mouth disease has put paid to the competition.

Badminton is the pinnacle of the sport of Three Day Eventing, which will be explained in more detail in the next chapter. In basic terms it is the test of all round horsemanship in three phases, with the rider on the same horse for all of these.

About 80 of the top horse/rider combinations in the world take part, and in terms of difficulty and challenge it supersedes the Olympic Games. The most popular day is Cross Country day, when the competitors tackle a fearsome four-mile course with over 30 solid and varied jumps.

As the numbers suggest it is a very spectator-friendly event, where children and dogs are welcome (the latter, and sometimes the former, on leads). There are also over 300 tented trade stands with 500 outlets, to cater for almost all shopping needs.

In *Badminton Revisited* (JR Books 2009) I gave a very personal account of the famous Trials. *Little Book of Badminton* is designed to be a pocket book containing history, profiles of some of the stars and people who make it all happen, how it has changed over the years, and how to enjoy it best as a fan or spectator. For obvious reasons the basic historical facts of both books are what they are, but the approach to my favourite subject is very different, and should be seen as a companion volume to those who have my first book on the subject, but more importantly a one-stop information repository for those who want to know what lies behind one of the world's great annual sporting 'Events'.

What is a Horse Trial?

The sport of Horse Trials, also known as Eventing, has its origins in the old cavalry schools of Europe at the end of the nineteenth century. It was once described by American general, Tupper Cole as 'A military event based on the duty of the officer courier who got through, or died.'

For the many centuries that horses were the main military form of transport, the need for correct training was imperative. As far back as 365 BC Xenophon wrote, 'As there will, doubtless, be times when the horse will need to race downhill and uphill and on sloping ground; times also, when he will need to leap across an obstacle, or take a flying leap from off a bank, or jump down from a height, the rider must teach and train himself and his horse to meet all emergencies. In this way the two will have a chance of saving each other.'

There were three distinctive attributes that had to be trained for, and which eventually became the basis of the competition to test this training.

First was the need to have the horse under control. If the rider couldn't achieve the basics of stop, start, left and right, a glorious, but futile death would be assured. This part of training has taken the name Dressage, which in its most elevated form is a type of ballet on horseback. Some of the more sophisticated moves, as demonstrated by

the Spanish Riding School in Vienna are in fact battle manoeuvres. The Levade, where the horse stands on its hind legs, protected the rider from a thrusting sword, and the Courbette, where the horse leaps into the air and kicks back, was designed to boot the opponent off his horse.

The second attribute needed was bravery and skill across country, as Xenophon described. For this, horses had to learn to trust their riders and the riders needed to train their horses to be fit for a long day's battle or march.

Finally the riders had to balance the need for speed and daring, with the responsibility to make sure they still had a sound animal to ride the following day.

The French can probably claim to have staged the first recognisable competitive three day event. In 1902 the Championnat du Cheval d'Armes was staged, for officers only. The obligatory set Dressage test, which was ridden on the first day, was a fairly simple one, but extra points could be gained in the optional

Left: *A Cavalry history*

Above: *Italian Cavalry test*

reprise libre, or free style. Some took this more seriously than others; suffice it to say that the overall winner of this stage offered a move known as shoulder in, serpentines up the arena, sideways canter, 180 degree turns on the back legs and also the front legs. In the canter he got the horse to lead with alternate legs, did the on the spot knees up movement, the Piaffe, then did it going backwards, did the Spanish walk forwards and backward, and finally a backwards canter.

Unsurprisingly to the British, more used to racing and hunting, this over keen interest in Dressage was described thus: 'The prevalent notion of the Continental horseman was somebody who spent his time bumming around an arena teasing his horse.' (Col. Hope, *The Horse Trials Story*).

It is the Cross Country phase which distinguishes Eventing from other equestrian sports. For both horse and rider the learning needs to start at a very novice level, with best results achieved when one part of the combination acts as school master to the other. An experienced rider will help a novice

horse, and a well trained horse will give a novice rider confidence.

The earliest report of Cross Country jumping instruction is that of the cavalry of King Charles XI of Sweden as they schooled over natural fences in 1688 to the instruction of the riding manual: 'When jumping a fence the rider will grab the mane, close his eyes and shout "Hey".'

The sport has had many names in its relatively short history. Until the 1980s it was still referred to on the continent as 'Le Militaire', although it had been open to civilians for many years. The military influence was still in evidence as late as 1981 when the main committee of the British Horse Society included no fewer than two generals, 13 colonels and 13 majors. The French have described it as 'L'épreuve au fond', the deepest test. The Swiss called it 'Gebrauchspferdeprufungen' and in Britain it was known somewhat prosaically as 'Combined Training', and its current alternative name, 'Horse Trials'.

Eventing has been an Olympic sport since Stockholm in 1912. (It

was suggested for London in 1908, but never materialised). The format took many goes to settle into the sport we know today. Competitors would go one at a time, with three or four minute intervals between each one. The Stockholm event was open to chargers and consisted of five tests over four days. This was the schedule: Saturday – Roads and Tracks Endurance (50km), Cross Country (5km); Monday – Steeplechase (3km); Tuesday – Show Jumping; Wednesday – Dressage.

The Games resumed after the Great War at Antwerp in 1920. Here there was no Dressage phase at all but two Endurance sections. Day one involved 45km Roads and Tracks and 5km Cross Country, followed by a day off. Then came a 20km Roads and Tracks followed by a 4km Steeplechase, another day off and finally the Show Jumping.

At Paris in 1924 the order we know now was introduced, but with days off between phases. The number of competitors made the Dressage stretch over two days followed by a bye day, then Roads and Tracks and Cross Country with a total distance of 36km, another bye day and finally Show Jumping. It is now universal that Dressage takes two days at the big events and there are no days off between, instigated at Amsterdam in 1928. From

this date the anomaly that Three Day Events last for four days was born.

As explained, Eventing started as a male, military, officer only sport, but now it is one of very few sports in which everyone – of any sex, rank and age – competes on the same terms. Before World War II, however, when it was still officer only, the Germans promoted their top rider Capt. Stubendorff, from the other ranks, so that he could ride in the Berlin Games, allowing him to take gold on Nurmi.

The next Games after the war were in London in 1948. This competition held on land between the two army towns of Aldershot and Sandhurst was

the catalyst which would lead first to the inaugural Badminton and then to an explosion of interest in the sport. It paved the way for Britain to become the Eventing centre of the world. In its post war infancy the sport became less widespread and The International Federation has succeeded over time to open it up to new emerging countries to join the established European, Antipodean and American participants. Many international riders, however, either base themselves in Britain, or spend some time here to take advantage of a well developed sport.

In a rather peculiar way the sport was created at elite level and has spread downwards. After the first Badminton in 1949, it was sensibly decided that some form of warm up competitions might be a good idea. The first public one day event was run by a stalwart of the British equestrian world, Henry Wynmalen on 29th March 1950. Britain now has five major three day events, Badminton, Burghley, Blenheim, Bramham and Blair Castle, and over 175 one day versions, spanning levels from advanced to tiny starter classes which are mainly patronised by hobby riders.

The scoring system is somewhat arcane. The Dressage test, rather like compulsory figures in ice skating, is performed in an arena in front of a judge or panel of judges, depending on the grade of competition. There are different routines for each level involving walking, trotting, halting, cantering in circles, serpentines, diagonals and a salute to the judge at the start and finish. The positive marks for each movement are then converted to a penalty, so the lowest score is the stage leader.

In Three Day Events the Cross Country comes next. The Endurance sections of Roads and Tracks and Steeplechase began to be phased out in 2005, and were gone by 2006, so riders now set off on a course of up to 6,840m which will include about 30 numbered jumps, some in combinations of two or three on a turn or down a dip. Unlike racing, the jumps change with each running and can include rails, logs, gates, walls, ponds and brush fences. These jumps don't knock down. Penalties are given for a refusal of the horse to jump, and elimination will occur with three stops at a single fence. In the past the old and bold used to remount after a fall and continue as a matter of pride. Safety concerns now mean a fall also means elimination. There is also an optimum time to complete the course, and penalties for going over it.

In the spirit of animal welfare, all the horses still in the competition get checked over before they are passed to take on the final Show Jumping. This is the phase which tests that the riders have left enough petrol in the tank to 'fight another day'. These coloured poles do knock down, and to keep tension right to the end, it is the overnight leader who jumps last. Many a big event has been lost in that final round as a pole hits the floor.

One of Eventing's unique aspects is that it takes both competitors and

organisers to fabulous parts of the countryside which would only otherwise be accessible by following hounds. Indeed the early competitors, when not from the army, tended to come from the hunting field.

The atmosphere is very friendly, as the sport relies on a large number of volunteers. Each jump on the Cross Country phase has a judge who will mark any faults. There are collecting ring stewards, commentators, grooms, score collectors and sport representatives.

The sport used to be the preserve of thoroughbred horses, but various cross breeds have been successful at the top level. At the more 'fun rider' level almost any breed will do. Children can get a taste of the sport at the national network of Pony Clubs, who run junior versions of the adult sport, though in recent years young riders on ponies have taken on the lower levels of the affiliated sport.

Turnout is important at all levels, and at the advanced end the Dressage uniform is top hat, cutaway tail coat and buff waistcoat. For Cross Country, riders choose their colour schemes for the shirt which will be worn with a body protector, and a silk covering for their crash hat. For the Jumping, a fitted jacket will be worn with a specialised Show Jumping helmet.

How it all Started

As touched on in the previous chapter, it was the Three Day Event at the London Games of 1948, held at Aldershot and Sandhurst that was the catalyst that brought Badminton to life. Britain was one of the few countries able to stage an, albeit Austerity, Games after the war. In 1947 the British Horse Society, then based in London, held a council meeting. It was to decide what equestrian teams to enter for the Olympic, and they settled on a Grand Prix Show Jumping team and a Three Day Event team for 1948.

Very few people had any idea what Eventing was in those days, and it was logical for a hunting and racing nation to avoid pure Dressage. A modest test at the Three Day Event would be manageable,

followed by Cross Country and Jumping, which was much more up Britain's street.

A Brigadier Bowden-Smith was one of the few people who had any experience of this type of competition, and was duly appointed Director of the Three Day Event. The 10th Duke of Beaufort was Vice-Patron and Vice-President of the International Equestrian Federation. His great friend Colonel Trevor Horn was asked to be one of the team selectors and also take on the duties of area manager for the Event. He went down to familiarise himself with the site and meet some of the riders, a full two weeks before the competition! He was to admit it was all very new to him.

The competition started on Wednesday

11th August with 46 competitors taking up the challenge in the now established format of Dressage first, followed by the Endurance and Cross Country and finally the Show Jumping. The first and last of these were contested at the Command Central Stadium at Aldershot, later known as Rushmore Arena. The Steeplechase part of the Endurance section was held at the Grand Military Racecourse, now better known to generations of point to point jockeys and event riders as Tweseldown.

The Roads and Tracks crossed the surrounding heath land between Sandhurst and Aldershot. The total distance covered on Cross Country day was 35km (22

miles) and the optimum time to complete this section was one hour, fifty minutes.

Being August, the organisers were worried about the temperatures, so the competition started at 6.00am, with the last one home in time for luncheon at 12.30. This was the first ever Three Day Event to be held in Britain, but there were high hopes for our team of three to do well on home ground, especially as Britain had secured a bronze in Berlin before the war.

There was a very mixed entry of nations including Turkey, Finland, Argentina and Mexico, but international participation began to decline once the sport had raised

BADMINTON

THREE DAYS' EVENT

THE MOST IMPORTANT

HORSE EVENT

IN GREAT BRITAIN

APRIL 20th, 21st & 22nd, 1949

1st Day—DRESSAGE, 10.30 a.m. at BADMINTON HOUSE.
2nd Day—SPEED & ENDURANCE, 14 miles, commence 2 p.m., including—
STEEPLECHASE COURSE (2 miles), DIDMARTON CAR PARK.
CROSS-COUNTRY (3 miles—21 Fences), BADMINTON CAR PARK.
3rd Day—JUMPING, 12 o'clock at BADMINTON HOUSE.
AND
TWO JUMPING COMPETITIONS (Organised by B.S.J.A.)—
TOUCH and OUT and OPEN COMPETITION.

ADMISSION to all Car Parks:

Motors, £1 per day. £2 10s., Seasons. Charabancs, £2 10s., 26 seaters.
Pedestrians 1s. each. ,, £3, 32 seaters.
Tickets may be had in advance on payment.

CATERING BY W. OSMOND & SONS, SALISBURY

Full information from: BRITISH HORSE SOCIETY, 16 Sloane Street, London, S.W.1.

W. S. Sales Ltd., Printers, Lewes

its game in subsequent years. It is really only recently that the sport has become as international as it was then. In those days all three riders' scores counted (now discards are permitted). For Great Britain Major Peter Borwick, riding Liberty, came seventeenth and Brigadier Lyndon Bolton came twenty-seventh with Sylvestre, despite sustaining two falls. Sadly though, Major Douglas Stewart and Dark Seal had to retire after the Steeplechase, so the team were eliminated and medal hopes dashed.

The team contest was won by the USA, with Sweden taking the silver and Mexico the bronze. Individual gold went to the aptly named Capt. Bernard Chevalier for France riding Aiglonne, silver to America's Lt. Colonel Frank Henry on Swing Low and Captain J. Robert Selfert and Claque, bronze for Sweden.

Watching the Event unfold with his involved great friend, Trevor Horn, was the 10th Duke of Beaufort. At a picnic lunch on Cross Country day, watching the riders take on the 35 obstacles, the Duke suggested that it might be a good idea to run something similar on an annual basis in an attempt to give British riders some match practice before the next Olympics at Helsinki.

Provided the idea had the backing

of the British Horse Society, the Duke would offer Badminton Park as the venue. He also had the inspired idea of asking the new expert, Trevor Horn, with all of two weeks' experience of the sport, to become the Event's first Director.

In the 10th Duke's own words, here is how the first Badminton came about: 'Knowing that the BHS wouldn't let us down we set to work immediately and started to advertise the Event for 1949 and to select the course. It was very much a two man affair in those days; Trevor used to put up the fences, I provided a very brilliant hunter. We used to make the top rail or two adjustable and I would go out and jump the fences. If the horse jumped them well we went ahead and decided that it was a suitable obstacle for a Three Day Event. And so we gradually worked it up, with our own point to point course for the Steeplechase part of the test. It was quite a job getting everything ready, and as a matter of fact Trevor did all the work, designed the course and built most of the jumps, being very much a one man show. He spent days here in the park on his own, working out the distances; of course the whole thing was a novelty to us, which made it a most interesting time.'

As was the way in those gentler amateur days, a committee was formed, which included Major Borwick, Britain's best performer at Aldershot, and a former amateur Grand National rider, Lt. Colonel 'Babe' Moseley.

Today, with the sport well established, there are quite a lot of people who could walk round a farm or estate and visualise a course on the ground, taking into account undulations and natural features. For Trevor Horn there were 1,500 acres in which to envisage a Cross Country course, an area for Steeplechase, a route for Roads and Tracks and somewhere to be the central show ground. The Endurance phase had to cover 14 miles (22km) and in those days there were five sections to be mapped out. Roads and Tracks, Steeplechase, which for some years used the local Beaufort Hunt point to point course, second Roads and Tracks, Cross Country and a 'warming down' run in.

To do this Colonel Horn walked, rode, cycled, and drove round the estate trying to imagine how it all might look the following April. His director's brief included recruiting an army of officials and helpers, which were largely locals from the Beaufort hunt, finding accommodation for the riders and also for the riders' grooms and indeed chauffeurs. (Today many riders

Far Left: *Poster for the first Badminton*

HOW IT ALL STARTED

*The final horse
inspection has
become a big
crowd pull*

live in their vast lorries).

Colonel Horn's head office was the top of his grand piano at his Gloucestershire home, though a great deal of the administration was done at the London offices of the British Horse Society, with some additional help from the Badminton estate office.

One thing the Event needed was publicity, as the only connection the public had with the name Badminton was the shuttlecock game, previously played in the Great Hall of the house. The first name given to the Event was the Badminton Three Days Event. However to establish that it was an equestrian competition the first posters bravely stated that it was: 'The Most Important Horse Event in Great Britain'. This was in a country which had staged the Grand National and Derby for many, many years and had also hosted international Jumping shows from the beginning of the twentieth century. The obvious advantage of having an event in a big park is that car parking was unlikely to be a problem, even if the organisers were able to muster up a crowd. Cars would be charged £1 a day, £2.10s for the whole event, and 'charabancs' £2.10s for twenty-six seaters and £3.00 for thirty seaters. People on foot paid a shilling.

As was to be a pattern for a long time, 20 of the 22 starters at the first Badminton, beginning on 29th April 1949, were from Great Britain. The other two were from Ireland. The competition had been instigated to help prepare British riders, though the invitation had been extended to the Irish, but there was little reason for continental competitors to make the trip for a contest that wasn't the Olympics. In these embryonic days there were no World or European Championships. In subsequent early years, as Badminton became the benchmark for the pinnacle of the sport, many foreign riders baulked at the challenge.

The 'hub' of the Event was sited in front of Badminton House, dominated by the Dressage arena, which had straw bales for spectator seats. The lack of continental Dressage talent rendered this phase something of a farce, and unpopular with the audience, who disliked seeing honest hunting type horses being asked, none too well, to perform 'circus tricks'.

The exception to the chaotic attempts was a professional riding instructor, Capt. Tony Collings and Remus, with a penalty score of 56. His 'pro' status made him ineligible for Olympic selection, so his fine efforts were of no interest to the selectors.

Another pro, John Shedden, was in third place, 34 points adrift, on the strong American thoroughbred Golden Willow.

The Cross Country course had been built by the estate head forester, Mr. Chappell, with what would today be considered rather flimsy timber. The 21 jumps were big but not too complicated, but there were banks, ditches, the lake, log piles and post and rail combinations, giving the riders a feel of a rather good run out hunting. That was in keeping with the cold and wet weather on the day. In Eventing the riders get to walk the course as many times as they want, though the horses see it for the first time in competition. On the first walk round many of the riders had nervous reservations about some of the obstacles, and surprisingly the organisers listened, and modified five of them. In more recent times events have a rider rep who will express competitors' concerns, and changes are still sometimes made.

Despite the jump modifications there were several falls, and eight competitors were eliminated for refusals on the course. The best jumping rounds, which may have surprised the hunting fraternity, came from two of the best Dressage performers, Collings and Shedden. In those days,

however, it was possible to reduce a bad Dressage score with a scorching Cross Country round, which S.C.M. Thompson and Guinea Fowl achieved by reducing a terrible first phase score, enough to put them second overnight. Sadly though, they withdrew before the Show Jumping phase. John Shedden was way in front overnight and Collings had a very expensive Show Jumping round to finish up sixth.

The penalty scores have altered many times over the years, but one show jump down in 1949 was a very expensive 10. Only one combination actually jumped clear, Ireland's Ian Dudgeon and Sea Lark, who came second to Badminton's first winner, John Shedden and Golden Willow.

Surprisingly there were five lady riders at that first Badminton, which was astounding considering only the previous year all at Aldershot had been male and, bar two, military.

The Most Important Horse Event in Great Britain actually made a profit of £20.00 and had persuaded a crowd of 6,000 to turn up over the three days. Badminton had entered the pantheon of great sporting weekends, seemingly fully formed at birth.

History of Badminton House

Family motto - *I Scorn To Change Or Fear*

Manor houses at Great and Little Badminton are mentioned in the Domesday Book under the amusingly different name of Madmintune. They had been in the Boteler family since 1275 and were sold to Edward, 4th Earl of Worcester in 1612. The family name of Beaufort originates with Katherine Swynford, mistress and later wife of John of Gaunt, third surviving son of Edward III. Her family chateau was Beaufort on the Upper Loire. John Beaufort was 1st Earl of Somerset, and thereafter they are Earls of Worcester until the 5th Earl was created 1st Marquess by Charles I.

In 1615 the 4th Earl gave Badminton to his son Sir Thomas Somerset (later in 1626 Viscount Cashel) who married the Dowager Duchess of Ormonde. Their unmarried daughter Elizabeth bequeathed Badminton to Henry Lord Herbert son of the 2nd Marquess. He became 3rd Marquis in 1667 and 1st Duke of Beaufort in 1682, the first of the long line of dukes. The family held vast tracts of land in Monmouthshire and Wales, where their principal castles were first Chepstow, then Raglan, before the 4th Earl moved to the richer lands east of the Severn.

The layout of Boteler's manor can still be discerned at Badminton today. It was approached from the south, past a stable block to the west through an arch on the

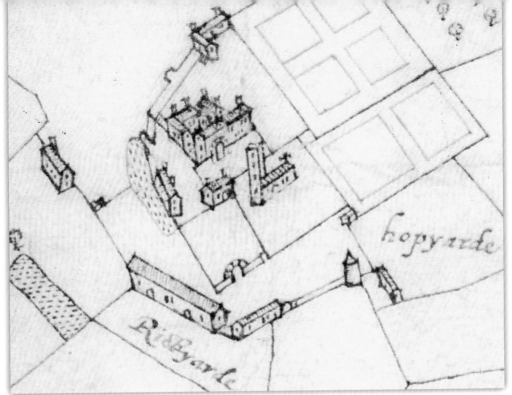

hopyarde

Ridyarde

site of the present stable arch, passing a medieval church on the right facing the south front. Opposite the west side was a stew pond, which is still there.

Sir Thomas Somerset moved into the house in 1617 and on becoming Lord Cashel set about modernising the Boteler house, principally creating two gabled facades looking into a courtyard with a cloistered ground floor. Of this early house, basement windows survive on the north, west and south fronts. The chronology of dating the fronts presents many problems. The north front is the principal one, its classical pilastered order exceptionally correct, probably dating

Above: *The House from a 1615 survey*

Right: *Entrance to the historic stable yard*

from about 1662 and suggestively by a London architect. Behind this is the Great Hall, in the 1st Duke's day for hanging tapestries.

In the 1st Duke's time the north front was only one room deep. From 1714 the second Duke added a full height corridor on the south side and improved internal communications. The 3rd Duke added a dining room on the site of Boteler's Great Hall and re-decorated the 1st Duke's Great Parlour, the work designed by Francis Smith. By 1730 Badminton House would be fairly recognisable with what we know today. Then, however, the house had a single central cupola and the north approach was paved, later replaced by gravel where the trot up now takes place.

In the courtyard on the west side of the house the 1st Duke had riding horse stables to the right of the clock arch, and his coaching stables to the left. The west elevation was almost certainly built for the 2nd Duke using his surveyor William Killigrew, and is shown on a survey of 1707 as nine windows across, fronting what was described as the New Hall, now divided up into several rooms. This was effectively the traditional entrance to the house. The Duke and Killigrew

also built the 2nd Duke's two pavilions, as Brewhouse and Laundry, to form a balanced vista, when seen from the Duchess's Orchard on the far side of the pond. The old kitchens to the right of the clock arch were also replaced by the Servants Hall, now festooned with antlers and used during the Three Day Event as a riders' and grooms' canteen. The north front was substantially altered by William Kent from 1745 for the 4th Duke, adding the twin domes, the eclectic pediment, and the north door, thus completing the eighteenth century project commemorated in 1750 in the paintings by Canaletto.

Badminton Village was a creation of the 2nd Duke and Killigrew, which was completed between 1710 and 1714 and is an integral part and tied extension of the main house, unlike most English houses of the time, which tended to be isolated in their parks. All the village houses are painted in a warm ochre, and many have crowned 'B' stone carvings, signifying the Beaufort Dukedom. The High Street is so fabulously unspoiled that it has been used in several film productions, with the village shop featuring in an edition of *Miss Marple*.

In 1819 the 6th Duke opened a new

approach to the house via Kennel Drive to avoid the village, to the left of which is the Dower House, once the old estate office. The gates came from Stoke Park, another Beaufort property near Bristol, in 1909, as did the gates at Village Lodge on the traditional entrance to the house.

A second phase of village development took place under the 8th Duke, roughly between 1850 and 1900. It was this Duke who revitalised the Beaufort Hunt and it was under his auspices that the huge square stable block, still used by the current hunt horses, but also for the competitors during the Trials, was built in 1878 by John D. Tait, the estate architect.

Tait was also responsible for the entrance porch-cochere on the west side.

Looking north through the Clock Arch and Cupola, by T. H. Wyatt and David Brandon, 1843, past the Coach Courtyard, sits one of Gibbs's Pavilions. Horses pass through this on their way to the park where all the Three Day Event competition takes place.

Also to the north there is a vast expanse of grass where the 3rd and 4th Dukes imagined a succession of temples, rotundas and obelisks, such as at Stowe. There was even to be a stone foot bridge over the landscaped lake. These all feature in the Canaletto view from the house,

LITTLE BOOK OF **BADMINTON**

but in fact were never built, as the family had debts after the unexpected premature death of the 3rd Duke in 1745.

Until the eighteenth century formal gardens were the accepted style and at Badminton the first Duchess had one laid to the east of the house. In 1752 the great leveller of formal gardens, Capability Brown, was consulted, but not taken on, however his follower, Nathaniel Richmond, was employed to landscape the park by the 5th Duke between 1776 and 1782. In 1841 the 7th Duke restored some formality of planting on the east again.

Boteler's park was only 60 acres but in 1657 it increased to 400. It was, however, in 1664 that Charles II gave the then 3rd Marquess of Worcester (the first Duke) permission to enclose another 1,400 acres. He loved trees and set about planting no fewer than 28 criss-crossing avenues spreading from the house. The spaces between provided enclosures for herds of various breeds of deer, of which 200 head of Red Deer currently inhabit the park.

Many of these avenues still exist, the most spectacular being The Great Avenue, which runs directly north from outside the deer park undulating to Worcester Lodge, visible two and a

HISTORY OF BADMINTON HOUSE

Right: *The servants' Hall as Grooms' canteen*

half miles from the house. The lodge was Kent's final great park building and was finished posthumously by Stephen Wright. Legend has it that a former Duke kept a mistress there, though there is no documented proof. Although this would be the grandest entry to Badminton and the iconic north facade, it was never used as a carriage drive to the Great House.

The main door on the north front opens into the Great Hall with its black and white marble floor. It was designed to accommodate the four great paintings by John Wootton – a celebration of the 3rd Duke's love for the horse and hunting. Over the chimney piece is a portrait of the 3rd Duke's favourite Arabian horse, Grey Barb. It was here that the game of Badminton was invented, and named as such, and was being played in the house from the 1830s.

Badminton House is very much a family home, and not generally open to the public although local history and architectural groups are welcomed on request. The Park hosts over 150,000 people annually for the Horse Trials and also hosts a number of charitable and other events.

Early Days

The 10th Duke's vision was to use the Horse Trials as a spring board for the British team's preparation for the Helsinki Games, so it was always envisaged that there would be at least four runnings, provided the first Event hadn't been a complete disaster. As Badminton was generally considered a success, preparations soon got underway for the 1950 Trials.

Again it was only open to Britain and Ireland and this time the latter sent three representatives to join the entry of 27 home riders. A year on, the Event was run in crisp spring sunshine and the reigning champion, John Shedden, set himself the then arduous task of entering both Golden Willow and

King Pin, ensuring that he would have to ride 32 competitive miles on Cross Country day.

Yet again, despite the fact that the Trials were being primarily run to find amateur Olympic prospects, it was the ineligible professionals who still showed the way. Tony Collings, now British team trainer, did far the best Dressage, again on Miss G.M. Christal's Remus, from lady rider Patsy Hildebrand and Lily, who were always good at this phase. John Shedden was a bit further down the line in this first phase with King Pin in sixth and Golden Willow in eighth, but as ever it was all to be fought out on the Cross Country. There were 28 mainly new fences on

the course, which again resembled a run out hunting, but with the added sensation that the rider was forever entering different hunt countries: one moment the Shires, the next the Cotswolds, with the dry stone walls, and then over the Irish Sea to Bank country. In the part of the course which is just in Wiltshire, an Irish bank was constructed, and is still used in modified form today. The strong pulling Golden Willow eschewed touching down the conventional way on the top, and famously jumped it in one.

After the Cross Country Shedden was leading with King Pin and was in sixth with Golden Willow, while in second was Capt. Arkwright with Lady Leigh's Minster Green. Tony Collings was in third with Remus. Whereas in the first running the top four after the Cross Country retained their positions in the Show Jumping, this time Remus emerged the winner with King Pin runner-up. Minster Green was third and the previous champion, Golden Willow coming up one spot to fifth. 1949's best female placing, Vivian Machin-Goodall, with her own Neptune, were bettered by one, as Miss Hildebrand finished fourth. A nail biting finish, a field of amateurs and professionals and top placed lady riders, Badminton 1950 was a template for all the subsequent excitement to come down the years.

News had obviously got out about The Most Important Horse Event. From the perfectly satisfactory first gate of 6,000, the organisers were able to post figures of 19,000 for the second running.

By 1951, with the Event established, the organisers opened the invitation to riders from further afield. Along with the 21 British entries there were two from the Netherlands, two again from Ireland and an unexpected eight horses and seven riders from Switzerland. The indoor, riding school-bound continental approach to equestrianism, compared to the open air, hunting-field modus of Britain and Ireland, was about to be tested. In a strange way the world has gone full circle, with many current riders starting as arena trained, and having to learn Cross Country skills, instead of being 'natural' at Cross Country and having to learn the refinements of arena craft. The Swiss weather had kept their horses under cover throughout the winter, so in April 1951 they had barely come out of hibernation.

By all accounts the third course at Badminton was considered to be the toughest yet, however, when walking the track the Swiss riders seemed remarkably unfazed. When asked why they were so cool, they are said to have replied, 'Because our horses are obedient.'!

Unsurprisingly they did well in the Dressage phase, producing the overnight leader Mahmud, ridden by Capt. Alfred Blaser, veterans of Aldershot 1948, where they had finished eleventh. Perhaps equally unsurprisingly, considering their build-up to Badminton, the Swiss horses seemed fat, unfit and not good in the wind. However they were 'obedient' and with sensitive horsemanship they coped perfectly well with the challenging course. A new fence, known as 'The Coffin' proved significant. It consisted of a rail, a slope down to a ditch, a slope up, and out over another rail. Not quite what the British might encounter out hunting, it caused a certain amount of carnage to the home riders. There were enough Swiss entries to have an informal team competition, which the visitors both won and came second in. Individual spoils went to Capt. Hans

Far Left: *Colonel Frank Weldon*

EARLY DAYS

Far Right: *The current Duke was second in 1959 with Countryman II*

Schwarzenbach and Vae Victis, with a British girl, fresh out of Pony Club, Jane Drummond-Hay, second on Happy Knight, and a Mr. Van Loon, from Holland, third with Nerantsoula.

It was a salutary lesson, however, for the British that they would have to work a bit on their training skills, and rely less on bravado, if they were going to put up a decent show in Helsinki the following year.

Badminton 1952 was ostensibly the culmination of the Duke's invitation to use Badminton as an Olympic spring board, but it was now firmly established in the sporting calendar. The continentals stayed at home for their Olympic preparations, so it was back to the British and Irish to take on the Gloucestershire challenge. The course was getting a bit longer. It was now up to four and a half miles long and had 34 numbered fences, with eight new ones including a jump at one of the quarries in the park. Making his riding debut was the commanding officer of the King's Troop RHA, Frank Weldon, who was to become such a Badminton 'name', both as a rider and subsequently as an inspired course designer.

The winner that year was Ireland's Capt. Mark Darley and Emily Little. The scores at the top were very tight, with the second-placed Dandy and Brian Young just two penalties behind, and Brigadier Lyndon Bolton, just another point five behind in third.

Another year with good weather helped bring in a bumper crowd which had now grown in a very short time to 55,000. The only unfortunate postscript was that our Olympic team was eliminated at Helsinki, so the original idea for Badminton hadn't quite worked out, but what had happened was that a truly fantastic sporting event had been created. In terms of kudos within the sport, Badminton's reputation was about to eclipse even the Olympic competition.

The enormous rise in interest in the sport of Eventing since the end of the war, starting with the Aldershot Olympics, and then the blossoming of Badminton, not only spawned one day warm up competitions of similar format, but also persuaded the International Equestrian Federation that there was enough interest on the continent to make a European Championships viable. These would initially be held in the three build-up years within the

Right: *The early layout*

Olympic cycle.

Badminton was chosen to run the Trials in what was to be Colonel Trevor Horn's swansong as director. Apart from the informal team competition in 1951, this was the only time that Badminton proper was to host an international championships. (There would be an anomaly two years hence at Windsor).

Only the Swiss, Irish and the British were able to field a team, which the home side duly won, as neither of the other two completed, but there were individuals from France, Holland and Sweden.

Riding as an individual for Great Britain, Major Laurence Rook took the title on Starlight XV from Frank Weldon with Kilbarry, with previous winner Hans Schwarzenbach and Vae Victis taking the bronze. Johan Asker from Sweden made his trip worthwhile, coming fourth with Iller. Three lady riders were in the top eleven: the redoubtable Vivian Machin-Goodall in fifth with Neptune, Audrey Huot, tenth with Sunbeam, and Veronica Pardoe eleventh with Garth Royal.

In the earlier days, and extending to the Mexico games of 1968, it was expected of people to lay down their horses for

their country. Many a good rider was 'jocked off' prior to a Championships, to let a 'more experienced man' take the ride. (Only men were eligible for International Championships until Basle in 1954). This happened to Margaret Hough, who stood down from Bambi V in 1952 to release the horse as an Olympic reserve and again in 1953 to let Bertie Hill take the ride to team gold at the 1953 Europeans.

Margaret led the Dressage from fellow lady rider Diana Mason with Tramella in second. The Cross Country course had a new fence, Trevor's Treble, suggested by Frank Weldon in a foretaste of his designing talent. It consisted of three fences in close formation on related distances. The idea that a ride round Badminton was akin to a top day's hunting was now a distant memory.

Weldon may well have won the Event had there not been a glitch with the timing on his Steeplechase round, but it was Margaret who became the first ever lady winner of Badminton, with Weldon second and Diana Mason third. The most remarkable result, however, was Ireland's Harry Freeman-Jackson who came fifth with Brown Sugar, a horse which had come second in the Irish Derby the week before the Horse Trials.

As a sort of coda to the first flowering years of Badminton, the 1955 Event transferred to Windsor, at the invitation of HM the Queen, where it again hosted a European Championships. This time five teams entered and there were 53 starters. There were no World Championships yet, so the European crown was open to the full range of international riders. Apart from representatives from GB and Ireland, Germany, Italy, Switzerland and Sweden, there were individuals from Australia, South Africa and Canada.

Great Britain convincingly won the team competition and Frank Weldon took the individual gold with Kilbarry. Silver went to a British individual, a rare naval officer in this sport, Commander John Oram, and bronze went to Bertie Hill with Countryman III. In the top ten after the medal winning British were Australian, Laurie Morgan, German, Otto Rothe, Swiss, Anton Buhler, Irish, Ian Dudgeon and Swede, Hans von Blixen-Finecke, to indicate just how international the sport could be, despite the fact that Britain was beginning to become the spiritual home of Horse Trials.

Far Left:
*Laurence Rook
and Starlight*

Stars:

Badminton's Best

Right from the very first Badminton only the very best all round riders and horses took up the challenge. The competition defeated, and continues to defeat, many of these experienced cavaliers, so to do well at this ultimate test is a great accolade; to actually win it puts the champion into the sport's history books.

There have been a handful of exceptional riders who have triumphed on more than one occasion and on more than one horse, and who deserve the accolade 'The Best of the Best'. There have also been one or two examples of amazing horsemanship at the Event, where a feat stays in the memory for all time.

Sheila Willcox (Waddington):

In 1955, almost unnoticed, an attractive young girl was entered at the 'Windsor' Badminton, with a horse called High and Mighty. She came a creditable thirteenth. The following year, back in Gloucestershire, the combination went into the lead in the Dressage, but were then overtaken by the reigning European Champion, Frank Weldon and Kilbarry by just 1.56 marks. Both finished on their Dressage scores and Weldon prevailed. A fierce rivalry ensued, fuelled perhaps by a frisson of chauvinism, snobbery and latent and unrequited lust.

In 1957 Kilbarry had been killed at a warm up event at Cottesbrooke, so Sheila

and High and Mighty started as favourites. Ignoring the old adage that a 'gentleman' must never be seen to be trying too hard, Willcox, from the start, adopted an unashamedly professional approach to her sport, and was not averse to a certain amount of gamesmanship. This time the combination led the Dressage phase, and with the slight advantage of being last in the draw, stormed round the course and jumped clear on the final day to win by a margin of 25.79 from Ireland's Penny Moreton and Red Sea. (Britain's Gillian Morrison was fourth with Benjamin Bunny, indicating that even if girls were still not eligible for the Olympics, they were right at the top of this sport).

By Badminton 1958 Sheila had become European Champion at Copenhagen the year before, and had been winning most of the One Day Events she had entered. Yet again she and High and Mighty led from the Dressage and were never caught. Married by 1959, Sheila Waddington entered Airs and Graces and duly became the only person in the history of the Event to win it three years running. In 1964, in the last of a six-year span when the competition (run over the same course) was split into Senior and Junior, points-based sections, Mrs.

Waddingon won 'Little Badminton' with Glenamoy. They were third in the 'Great' section the following year. In 1968 Sheila came thirteenth with Fair and Square and retired that horse on the Cross Country at her last appearance in 1969.

Sheila's competitive career ended when she broke her back in a fall at the Tidworth Three Day Event, but she continued to teach, and wrote the first instructional manual on the sport.

Richard Meade:

Richard probably spans the time between the pioneer days of Horse Trials to what many think of as one of the Golden Ages of the sport. He first came to Badminton in 1963, when the dreadful winter and spring forced the organisers to run Badminton as a One Day Event. Riding Barbarry, Richard came second on a day of driving rain and deep going. They were thirteenth the following year when it was a proper Three Day Event again.

In 1967 he returned with Turnstone to come sixth, and the pair were second to Jane Bullen on the pony Our Nobby, in 1968. At the Mexico Olympics that year he was gifted the ride on an injured

Far Left: *Richard Meade and The Poacher*

Mary Gordon-Watson's Cornishman V to pick up a team gold alongside Ben Jones who had the ride on Martin Whiteley's The Poacher. As unofficial British team captain Richard had the pick of rides in those days and by 1970 was in the saddle of Whiteley's horse. He didn't waste the opportunity and duly took the Badminton title.

The following year he had a workmanlike round on Flamingo and came back in the Olympic run-up on Laurieston. He should have won that too, but being over cautious as last to go, in the lead, on Show Jumping day he went clear over the fences but picked up 1.25 time faults, to hand the prize to Mark Phillips and Great Ovation. At least Richard had the satisfaction of winning the individual, and team gold medals at Munich later in the year. Richard was second again at Badminton the following year on a chance ride with Bar Hammond's Eagle Rock.

In 1980 Richard took on another Gordon-Watson ride, Speculator II, but withdrew before the Jumping. In 1981 he completed with Speculator in thirty-secondth place, but came third with Kilcashel that year. It was therefore somewhat against past form that

Speculator, with Richard at the helm, won the trophy in 1982.

Richard has passed on the baton to his son Harry, who has had several successful Badminton rides. Meade Senior acts as an expert equestrian witness in court.

Jane Bullen (Holderness-Roddam):

The Bullen family had been steeped in Showing, with Jane and her sister Jenny seen at all the top venues. Older brother Mike had already become a Badminton stalwart and ridden at the Tokyo Olympics. Jane first came to Badminton with the diminutive Our Nobby in 1967 and managed to come fifth. Next year was Olympic year, and in those days the Badminton course was racked up a notch to help the selectors. The first and only lady rider to date to ride at the Olympics had been Lana Dupont of the USA, who had completed four years previously. Undeterred, Jane, who was a student nurse in London at the time, had the ride of her life and won Badminton at her second attempt. She was duly selected for Mexico and was part of the gold medal-winning team.

Jane had a few other rides: Western Morn in 1973 and Devil's Jump and

LITTLE BOOK OF **BADMINTON**

Troijoy in 1976; but her next real prospect was the American-owned Warrior, on which she came fourth in 1977. Ten years after her win on Our Nobby, she triumphed again.

Jane has written many books on horses and has held high office on many committees and boards. She runs the successful West Kington Stud and is also one of Princess Anne's Ladies in Waiting. In the 1977 film *International Velvet*, Jane and Warrior doubled for Hollywood star Tatum O'Neal and her horse. The film was about a young English girl making it to an Olympic gold against the odds; effectively Jane's own story.

Mark Phillips:

In 1968 a young Officer Cadet, taking leave from Sandhurst, marked his card by coming an impressive fourth at his first attempt on Rock On, in a year when only 24 of the 55 starters completed the Event. The days of Army dominance in the ranks of competitors was gone, but Mark Phillips returned to Badminton as a Lieutenant in 1971 with his Aunt Flavia's Great Ovation. They did the best Dressage and achieved the second-fastest Cross Country round to lift the

Whitbread trophy for the first time. They successfully defended their title the following year, despite the fact that it took much of Mark's skill to produce these results from not the most genuine horse to win a major prize. In 1973 they retired before the Cross Country and in 1974 the horse threw the towel in and was eliminated.

By this stage Mark had married Princess Anne and had taken on the ride on the Queen's strong, grey Columbus. After performing one of the best Dressage tests, they were only one of six combinations to go clear inside the time and won by a near 13-point margin.

In 1976 he was third on a horse called Favour and had two other rides with Brazil and possibly his 'best' horse, Persian Holiday, neither of whom completed. As noted in the Royal section, later in the book, he deputised for Princess Anne in 1977 with Goodwill coming fourteenth, but retired the unlucky Persian Holiday on the Cross Country. He was third on Columbus in 1979 and in 1980 he was sixth on Lincoln, but had to retire Columbus on the Cross Country.

Returning in 1981, Mark won on Lincoln from his future second wife, Sandy Pflueger, in a year when 63 of the

80 starters completed the Event but yet again he had to pull up Persian Holiday.

Mark became the US team trainer for many years and is one of the world's top course designers, whose portfolio includes Burghley and the British Open courses at Gatcombe Park.

Lucinda Prior-Palmer (Green):

Emerging from the Royal Artillery Pony Club and Britain's gold-winning Junior team of 1971, the primrose Cross Country colours of Viceroy's granddaughter, Lucinda Prior-Palmer, made their debut at Badminton in 1972 aboard Be Fair, where the combination also made an impressive debut to finish fifth.

The next year, after a good Dressage, Lucinda and Be Fair won by over 21 penalties from Richard Meade, reigning individual Olympic champion, and Eagle Rock.

Their return in 1974 was a disaster, with a stop at the Quarry and a fall at an S fence early on the course. Undeterred, Lucinda returned after the void year of 1975 with a horse called Wideawake, which had taken her some time to get attuned to. Nevertheless, over a fairly stiff course, which would have been used the previous year, they prevailed and beat future Badminton director Hugh Thomas on his own Playamar.

There was, however, a tragic postscript when, just before doing the individual lap of honour after the prize giving, Wideawake reared up and dropped down dead.

Matt Straker had completed Badminton with George in 1973 and 1974 and in 1976, with Matt on Army duty, the ride went to Canadian, Robert Desourdy, who completed. Lucinda was put up in 1977. She was a bit apprehensive as the horse had fallen on his last five outings. However in Lucinda's hands all was well and she won for the third time, coming third for good measure on the rather one-paced, but honest Killaire.

In 1978 it might have been her fourth Whitbread trophy, but Lucinda was pipped to second on Village Gossip, by Jane Holderness-Roddam, posting her second win 20 years after winning as Jane Bullen on Our Nobby.

Killaire, however, had his moment in the limelight by winning in 1979 from Monacle and Sue (Hatherly) Benson. Sue was to go on to design the Cross Country course for the Greenwich Olympics in

2012. Lucinda and Killaire were runners-up in 1980 to Mark Todd, an unknown New Zealand dairy farmer, on Southern Comfort. Killaire and Lucinda had a unique record of coming first, second and third at the ultimate Event. They were also tenth in 1981.

In 1982, on two new rides, Lucinda came seventh on Regal Realm and eighth with Beagle Bay, only to win with Regal Realm the next year. For good measure Beagle Bay was fifth. Lucinda had now won Badminton a record five times.

Remarkably, back she came to take the 1984 title on Beagle Bay for her sixth win (with Village Gossip in fifth) to complete the most remarkable Badminton career of them all.

Lucinda now teaches Cross Country riding internationally and commentates for TV.

Virginia Holgate (Leng, Elliot):

In 1972, as a girl with model looks, Ginny Holgate was just one of the numbers when the Junior European Championships were held at Eridge in England, where she came an unspectacular nineteenth with Dubonnet. The following year, however, the pair were crowned Junior Champions at Pompadour in France.

Ginny's rise to the top of Eventing was far from conventional. The early part of her life was spent in all corners of the globe, where her father was serving with the Royal Marines. She was born in Malta, the family moved to Cyprus and then Canada before settling in Kent when Ginny was three. Ginny started riding then, but soon the family were on the move again to Singapore, where her redoubtable mother, Heather, became a stalwart of the Pony Club. After a stint back home, and boarding school, the family were off to Manila. As they were about to depart Heather's father produced a weedy six-month old colt, costing £35.00. Heather named all her horses after drinks, and this was Dubonnet.

When time had passed Ginny and Dubonnet were ready for competition. It didn't start well. They were eliminated for three refusals at their first little jumping show.

They were also eliminated at their first event in 1971. In her first Pony Club team outing she started the jumping round before the bell had rung, and eliminated her entire team, then at her first official adult event she and Dubonnet

Far Left: *Ginny Leng and Master Craftsman*

Far Right:
Ian Stark and Glenburnie

jumped fine but missed out two fences on the Cross Country and were eliminated again. Of this Champions are made.

The pair first entered Badminton and came an unspectacular thirty-first. The last reigning British Junior European Champion to come straight to Badminton was Richard Walker who duly won it in 1969 to become the youngest ever winner at 18 with Pasha.

In 1975 Ginny won the Montreal Olympic test event on her second string, Jason, and then took a bit of the winter off, working in the tie department at Harrods.

There were high hopes for the 1976 season, then disaster struck. At the Ermington One Day Event Ginny had a crashing fall and broke her arm in 23 places. Amputation was seriously considered, however, with the skill of the surgeons, and five operations later, Ginny was able to ride Tio Pepe at Burghley six months after the fall. The dream comeback was marred when Ginny missed out a fence in the jumping to eliminate herself yet again!

The bad luck persisted when Tio Pepe 'broke down' on the Steeplechase at Badminton in 1978. The only thing to lighten the gloom had been several weeks in September and October 1977, being one of the action riders on the feature film *International Velvet*.

At the start of 1978 Heather had two promising youngsters in Priceless and Night Cap. By 1981 Priceless was ready for Badminton and duly came eighth. The second launch of Ginny's career was underway. They did better the following year, coming fourth. Ginny was eleventh in 1983 with Night Cap and completed with him in 1984. Priceless went to the Los Angeles Olympics and won team silver and individual bronze, having previously picked up World and European Team golds.

At Badminton 1985 it all came together and Ginny won the Event with Priceless and came third with Night Cap. Night Cap was fourth the following year. That year she won Burghley on a strong pulling grey, Murphy Himself, but later surrendered the ride in a swap to Ian Stark after a very hairy ride at Badminton in 1988, which left Ginny on the deck.

Ginny's next star emerged on the national circuit in the year Badminton was cancelled in 1987. Master Craftsman came third at Badminton in 1988 and won a team silver and individual bronze at the Seoul Olympics. They came back to win Badminton 1989, before becoming individual European Champion the same year.

Master Craftsman was second at Badminton in 1992, but Ginny had had a heavy fall from Welton Houdini that year at the rails at the Fairbanks Drop. She got his confidence back by hunting him all season and entered him as her only Badminton ride in 1993. They finished on their Dressage score to win from the front.

Ginny has subsequently been trainer of the Irish Olympic squad.

Ian Stark:

Ian's was a remarkable rise to the top of his sport. For many years he had been gainfully, if boringly, employed as a DHSS clerk, married with two small children and a minor interest in horses. After a holiday he decided, with the surprising encouragement of his wife, Jenny, to chuck it all in and become an eventer. His early horizons were limited, since events in Scotland are few and far between, and he was many miles away from the mainstream centre of the sport south of the border.

Having decided on his quest, initially supported by family capital, Ian and Jenny

came down to recce the ultimate goal of Badminton in 1975. The tribulations of the sport were particularly in evidence that year as the Trials were rained off after the Dressage. They came to watch again in 1976 but decided not to return until their visit would be a rehearsal for the real thing.

With his two top horses now established six years hence, the Starks decided 1983 would be the year for a final look. Just a few weeks later Ian had won the Bramham Three day Event in Yorkshire with Sir Wattie and was third on Oxford Blue.

1984 would be the year when the 'unknown' Ian Stark was to arrive. Just like Sheila, Mark, Lucinda, and in her second coming, Ginny, the debut was a portent of things to come. Ian was third with Oxford Blue and sixth with Sir Wattie. 1985 wasn't so auspicious. Oxford Blue was only twenty-fifth and Ian was eliminated on Lairdstown. It all came right, however, in 1986, one of the very wet years, when he won with Sir Wattie by nearly 10 penalties from Rachel Hunt and Piglet II.

Badminton fell victim once again to the weather in 1987, but on battle commencing in the new month of May in 1988, Ian achieved the only ever one, two with Sir Wattie and Glenburnie.

Having taken over the Ginny Leng ride on Murphy Himself, the pair came second in 1991.

In 1996 Ian was in pole position on the final day with Stanwick Ghost only to lose it in the Show Jumping. And history repeated itself the following year when they had five down to throw it away.

Ian's winning ways were not over, however, as he came back to take the title again in 1999 with Lady Hartington's Jaybee.

With his DHSS days an improbable back story, Ian, always the daredevil, now has a pilot's licence and is an emerging international course designer, responsible for the track at the site of his first triumph, Bramham.

Mary Thomson (King):

Mary Thomson had no equestrian past whatsoever, but nevertheless became a horse-mad child, doing all sorts of odd jobs to support her hobby. What, however, put her on the road to stardom was a stint at what can only be described as the boot camp discipline surroundings of Badminton's first serial winner, Sheila

Willcox. It may not have been a laugh a minute, but it instilled in Mary all the attention to detail and dedication that were to take her right to the top.

At Badminton 1989 she felt she had been harshly marked in the Dressage with King Boris, as one judge had consistently given her lower scores than the other two, and despite having a great Event, finished on her Dressage score less than one fence behind the winner, Ginny Leng and Master Craftsman. The following year the pair were third behind surprise winner Nicky McIrvine on Middle Road.

In 1991 Mary and Boris led the Dressage by five penalties from Helen Bell and Troubleshooter. She was also in fifth on her other ride, King William. (Most of Mary's horses have the prefix King).

Sadly it all went pear-shaped on Cross Country day, with Boris giving the crowd its money's worth by depositing Mary in the Lake and King William slipping up on the flat in Huntsman's Close and incurring 60 penalties.

1992 was another of the wet and windy years, making the Cross Country more challenging than usual, and only 21 jumped round clear and none got close to the optimum time. Mary had come so close to winning with Boris, but it was King William that won her the first ever Mitsubishi Motors Trophy. King William had been one of three horses sculptor, Judy Boyt, had based her trophy design on.

In 1996 Mary fell at the first fence on her second ride Star Appeal and was so stiff the next morning she retired King William on the final day despite a good performance and almost certain placing.

The 1997 entry was a massive 151, of which only a maximum of about 90 could start. Star Appeal cleared the first fence this time, and indeed all the others, to lie third on the final morning and move up to runner-up spot to America's David O'Connor and Custom Made after Ian Stark's disaster with Stanwick Ghost.

In 2000 Mary's faith in Star Appeal was vindicated when he won Mary her second Badminton title. Mary broke her neck in a fall in 2001 but made a remarkably quick recovery to come third at Burghley the following year with King Solomon.

At the time of writing in 2013 Mary had contested six Olympic Games back to back, and was still competing. She now breeds many of her rides, while her daughter Emily has made her Junior international debut.

Pippa Nolan (Funnell):

Pippa came up through the ranks of Juniors, winning gold medals on the way. She made her Badminton debut in 1988 on Sir Barnaby, completing in twenty-seventh place. Similarly to Ginny Leng, her Junior ride gave her a taste of the ultimate challenge, but it would take a couple of real Senior horses to convert junior promise into senior results. Pippa found these with Supreme Rock and Primmore's Pride.

At the 2002 Event Pippa and Supreme Rock were reigning European Champions and were second last to go of the 87 starters, going in with a Dressage lead of six points. The course that year was very twisty and technical, something that wouldn't usually suit the rangy 'Rocky'. This led to her incurring 5.2 time penalties, minimising her lead to a whisker. The pressure was taken away a bit in the jumping as her close rival Andrew Hoy with Darien Powers had four down. She had a fence in hand from William Fox-Pitt, kept her nerve to jump clear, with a single time penalty, to take the title.

The following year Pippa cut it even finer. Her closest rival, Pia Pantsu,

Far Left: *Mark Todd and Southern Comfort*

jumped clear to finish on 44.4. Pippa, on 34 had two fences in hand. She knocked one, so then went so cautiously she incurred six time penalties. She squeaked it by just point four of a penalty.

2004 was a year to forget for Pippa. She was shot out of the saddle when Viceroy clobbered the Gate at Huntsman's Close and taken to hospital for a checkup. She then came back to Badminton, in the second last year of the long format, to set off on the Endurance phase with Cornerman. Pippa then had an identical fall from her second ride.

Putting this behind her, Pippa came to Badminton with Primmore's Pride the next time, joint favourite at the bookies with William Fox-Pitt, the 2004 winner. Primmore's Pride had won Kentucky the previous year and had won Burghley to secure Pippa the elusive Rolex Grand Slam for a rider winning Kentucky, Burghley and Badminton in a row.

Both William and Pippa had day two Dressage tests and Pippa emerged just in front. Going into the final jumping Pippa had a lead of just 1.6. She kept her nerve to take her third title. Her three wins were by an added total of just six penalties. This was a far cry from the record gap between first and second, achieved by Anneli Drummond-Hay and Merely-a-Monarch who beat Frank Weldon by 42 penalties in 1962!

Pippa is married to top international Show Jumper, William Funnell, and has written a series of children's books, *Tilly's Pony Tails*. She has also helped develop a range of computer games that bear her name (though not always her likeness!).

Sir Mark Todd:

In 1980 an unheralded New Zealand farmer, Mark Todd, arrived for his first Badminton. It was one of the years when the course was a true Weldon frightener. The most significant fence was a Foot Bridge, slung at an angle over the Vicarage Ditch. It caused several falls, and the course in general caused lots of problems all the way round. Only 29 of the 68 starters completed the Event. If ever there was a year when a bit of Cross Country luck was needed this was it. Mark's horse Southern Comfort spread-eagled on landing at the Foot Bridge, but their momentum skidded them back to an upright position and they continued on their way without a fault.

Mark, and future British team trainer, Goran 'Yogi' Breisner were the only two to complete the course inside the time. With a clear Show Jumping on the final day, and last to go Lucinda Prior-Palmer and Killaire rolling a pole, Mark became the first Badminton debutant to win since Richard Walker in 1969.

Mark returned in 1983 to come ninth on Felix Too, but was back properly in the limelight coming second to Lucinda in 1984 with the tiny Charisma IV. That year the pair went on to take individual gold at the Los Angeles Olympics. At Badminton after the Games, Mark and Charisma IV came second to Ginny and Priceless by just one point. In 1986 he was fifth with Any Chance.

Mark and Charisma IV won individual gold again at the Seoul Olympics in 1988, but at Badminton 1989, deputising for Rodney Powell, he rode The Irishman and came third, showing his skill as a substitute jockey.

By 1994 Lynne Bevan, a pure Show Jumper by inclination, had ridden Horton Point happily round Badminton three times, but a week before the Event had broken her collar bone in a fall. Mark had trained Lynne a bit and liked the horse. He seemed the natural choice of last-minute replacement.

Since Mark was also entered on another horse, Just an Ace, he would have a late and early draw. As it turned out Horton Point was drawn number one. Lynne had never really put her foot down speed-wise on the Cross Country, but no one expected Todd to hang around. He set the standard and could only have been bettered later in the day by German rider, Marina Loheit, but she fell leaving Mark overnight leader and eventual winner. The Bevans retired the horse after the triumph and Lynne went on to win one of Show Jumping's top prizes, the Queen Elizabeth Cup on a horse with which Mark, no mean pure Show Jumper himself, had had a disappointing show at Hickstead in 1997.

In 1995 Mark rode former Nick Burton mount, Bertie Blunt, but the horse failed the final trot up. During the following year Mark lost the ride after a disagreement with one of his sponsors and the horse was put on the market. When it failed to sell two of his other owners sent it back to Mark.

On the final day of the 1996 Event Mark and Bertie Blunt were in third. They went clear to retain that position and sat it out as the last two went in to jump. David O'Connor had one down to drop to third behind Vaughn Jefferis and Bounce. Last to go was Ian Stark and Stanwick Ghost who dropped to sixth with two down, and Mark had posted his third Badminton title. Before heading for retirement Mark also managed two more second placings with Broadcast News in 1998 and Word for Word in 1999.

Mark returned to New Zealand and trained racehorses successfully, until, almost jokingly, someone suggested to him that he might consider coming out of retirement to have a go at the Bejing (Hong Kong) Olympics in 2008. The 'joke' worked and Mark was back enjoying the sport for a second time. He decided to move back to Britain again. In 2012 Mark entered NZB Land Vision at Badminton and to popular acclaim won his fourth title a decade after his retirement. He is the oldest rider to win Badminton at 55. (The youngest was Richard Walker who won aged 18 with Pasha in 1969).

Todd was awarded a Knighthood in the 2013 New Year Honours, the only equestrian to receive the highest accolade.

All the above have been the best of the best at Badminton, making up the Hall of Fame of multiple winners. There are also three other riders, one who won once, one who could still win and one who achieved immortality two ways. Their feats deserve mention.

Bill Roycroft:

Bill, a wiry Australian farmer, was part of his country's raiding party en route to the Rome Olympics in 1960, where they carried all before them. Bill won Badminton that year on Our Solo, from his countryman Laurie Morgan and Salad Days. However it was in 1965 that he made history by entering and completing on three different horses, Eldorado, second in the senior section, Stoney Crossing who was sixth and Avatar, who was second in the Little Badminton section. He would have competed for roughly 45 miles and been in the saddle for three hours.

Lorna Sutherland (Clarke):

In 1970 Lorna Sutherland, well known for her success on her two coloured horses, Popadom and Gypsy Flame, emulated Roycroft's feat with her 'circus ponies' and The Dark Horse. The rule was changed later in the long format era to restrict riders to two horses only, so the marathon ride was never completed again.

Lorna, who first rode at Badminton in 1967, coming eighth with Nicholas Nickelby, finally hung up her boots in 1992 after a then record 22 completions of the Great Event. She then spent many years commentating on the Event for BBC TV.

Andrew Nicholson:

New Zealand's Andrew Nicholson first rode at Badminton in 1984 and completed with Kahlua and Rubin. The closest he came to winning was in 2004 with Lord Killinghurst, when he was runner-up. He has won Burghley several times, but has the probably unassailable record of 31 completions on 18 different horses, and is still riding as this goes to press.

Every horse that completes Badminton is a hero to its connections, and some have been fantastic servants who have provided thrills year after year.

Over 30 have been round four times; about 20 have done five, but four special horses managed six completions: Merry Sovereign and Clissy Strachan in 76, 77, 78, 79, 80, 81; Get Smart and Karen Dixon in 88, 89, 90, 91, 93, 94; Troubleshooter and Helen Bell in 90, 91, 92, 93, 94, 96 and Spring Along with Daisy Berkley in 04, 05, 06, 08, 09, 10.

It must be pointed out, without in any way detracting from the achievement, that any completions after 2005 were without the Endurance phases, so really a One Day Event run over a leisurely three days, albeit with a longish Cross Country.

There are four horses that have completed the Event seven times. All but one of Caroline Powell's Lenamore's rounds were post-2005, in 06, 07, 08, 09, 10, 11; James Robinson's Comanche has three in long format, 03, 04, 05 and four in short, 06, 09, 10, 11; Jeanette Brakewell's Over to You, five long, two short, 98, 99, 03, 04, 05, 06, 07.

The only horse to have completed the Event seven times, all in long format, was Ballycotton, who went round from 1990 to 95, inclusively, with Andrew Harris and once with Sarah Longshaw in 1997.

Left: *Bill Roycroft*
and his three

65

Royals at Badminton

Badminton has had interest from the Royal family from the early days. The house and Beaufort family were familiar to the Windsors, since Queen Mary spent the years of the Second World War staying with the 10th Duke and his Duchess, Mary.

1952, the fourth running of the Event, was the first time that the Queen came to watch the Horse Trials, along with the Duke of Edinburgh and Princess Margaret. She had a drive round the course the day before the Cross Country and watched all the action from the vantage point of hay wagons, or sitting with her hosts on rugs, right amongst the general public. While watching at the water jump she retrieved the riding whip

of a soaking Olympic hopeful.

When visiting the Event the Queen, a keen horsewoman, and the Royal Party would go out for a morning ride before the competition started, and would present the prizes in the afternoon of the final day.

At the second Badminton in 1950, two of the competitors were to have later royal links. Major Dick Hern came eleventh that year and rode at the Event another three times in a row. He went on to become the Queen's principal racehorse trainer. Also riding for the first time that year was Major John Miller, who came sixteenth that year and seventh in 1951. He was later to become Crown Equerry. In that role Miller was

in charge of the Royal Mews, and all the Queen's carriages. Most importantly, however, he was instrumental in introducing a potentially bored Princess Anne to the sport of Eventing.

She became a member of the Garth Pony Club and through the now 'Sir' John's organisation, hosted some invitational drag hunts for other local Pony Club children. The Princess then started being trained by Alison Oliver, wife of top post-war show jumper, Alan Oliver, and made her first appearance at Badminton in 1971 on the home bred chestnut gelding, Doublet.

Despite being harassed by photographers before her test, and inducing her to come out with the classic and now famous admonishment of 'Naff Off', she performed the second best Dressage behind her future husband Mark Phillips. For some reason she held the brake on too much on the Steeplechase phase and picked up a totally unnecessary 32 penalties, without which she could have retained her second place, despite one show jump down, but nevertheless finished a very creditable fifth at her first attempt.

That autumn she was to become European Champion on Doublet at Burghley, and her appearance at the top two Three Day Events in one year boosted the sport into the spotlight, from where, by and large it has remained ever since.

Above: *Princess Margaret between the 10th and 11th Duke of Beaufort*

The Princess's next appearance at Badminton was in 1973, this time on a horse called Goodwill. The course that year was arguably the most difficult ever built at Badminton and more than half the competitors failed to complete. However Princess Anne and Goodwill got into the money, coming eighth in the year that Lucinda Prior-Palmer won for the first time. That autumn at the Europeans at Kiev, then in the Soviet Union, the pair, going as individuals, had a crashing fall at the notorious second fence. The same year the Princess had been riding Columbus, a very strong, grey gelding belonging to the Queen. Deciding the horse was more of a man's ride, it was agreed that Mark Phillips should take it on.

After the carnage of 1973, the 1974 course was definitely on the kinder side as the 60 starters formed up. It was to be a bit of a curate's egg Royal performance. Doublet did the best Dressage, but fell on the Steeplechase and retired, while Mark Phillip's previous winner, Great

Ovation, never the most genuine horse, threw in the towel and was eliminated on the Cross Country. Goodwill meanwhile came fourth, with the Princess on board and Mark conjured a superb round out of Columbus to finish on their Dressage score and receive the Whitbread Trophy from the horse's owner, the Queen.

Goodwill, who had won the individual silver medal at the European Championships at Luhmuhlen in 1975, reappeared in 1977 with Mark Phillips in the saddle, as the Princess was pregnant with Peter, and they came fourteenth.

Back at Badminton in 1978, this was the first time the Princess was out of the prizes, finishing sixteenth on Goodwill, but they came back to be sixth in 1979, adding to their collection of silver horse replica trophies.

Columbus had sustained a serious injury on completing the course at the 1974 World Championships at Burghley, but perhaps surprisingly lined up in 1980, only to pull up on the Cross Country and retire permanently.

Princess Anne's final competitive Badminton entry was in 1982 with the chestnut Stevie B. Eleven years after her debut, with an enviable result sheet, the Royal rider sportingly gave the crowd and TV audience what they had secretly been waiting for: a comprehensive ducking in the Lake. It was to mark a pause in active Royal participation at Badminton, and indeed from the turn of the decade, Her Majesty no longer came to the Event.

The Royal link remained however, as The Queen Mother came to present the prizes in 1982 and 1983 and Princess Michael of Kent, a keen rider, who lived locally to Badminton performed the duty several times during that period. In 1991 Diana Princess of Wales did the honours with Princes William and Harry in tow and the Queen returned in 1999 for the 50th anniversary running of the Event.

Only six years after this, Princess Anne's daughter, Zara Phillips, had quietly risen up through the younger rider ranks, and without yet riding

at Badminton had been crowned European Champion at Blenheim in 2005, thus emulating her mother, and then going one better the following year by taking the World title on her own Toytown at Aachen.

Zara emulated Princess Anne by being awarded the BBC Sports Personality of the Year and went on to win team silver at the Greenwich Event during the London Olympics in 2012.

The media were waiting for her debut at the world's premier Event

and she was duly entered in 2007. The media circus started all over again. It was just like the Princess Anne days, except that the photographers seemed much better behaved than they had been in the Seventies, even helping to control the over keen public snappers with their phone cameras. The ground conditions that year were not good and many riders, including Zara opted to withdraw from the competition after the Dressage phase.

In 2008 Zara came with two horses, Glenbuck, who came sixteenth and

Ardsfield Magic Star, nineteenth, so she broke her Badminton duck with two completions. The next year wasn't so good, when she had to retire Toytown on his only full attempt and also failed to complete on Ardsfield Magic Star, but completed with penalties on Glenbuck in 2010 to finish forty-eighth.

Her presence to date kept the papers happy, because she had provided a 'telegenic' fall and also had the travelling supporters' club of Princes Harry and William, with Kate Middleton in the crowds as well.

In 2012 Badminton was thrilled to have invited Prince William and the Duchess of Cambridge to present the prizes, only for the Event to suffer one of its very rare cancellations.

Badminton has always welcomed a vast and mixed crowd, but is very proud of its Royal cachet and the relaxed involvement of the Royal Family as guests, competitors and general spectators.

LITTLE BOOK OF **BADMINTON**

Changes

In its 60 plus years of existence Badminton has been in a constant state of evolvement. Since Three Day Events were initially solely held at Olympic Games, it was inevitable that each Cross Country course would be different, and competitors would have to be ready for a new challenge each time. Since Badminton was the first Event to run on an annual basis it would have been easy to keep the course the same each year, as it has been (with modifications) to the Grand National and more recently the Hickstead (Show Jumping) Derby. However, as it had been set up primarily as an Olympic practice, it made sense to have a different challenge each year. For a long time, the course was a bit easier the year after the Games, and got increasingly difficult during the Olympic cycle. This became unnecessary when eventually Badminton became more difficult than the Olympics, and also there were alternating World and European Championships in non-Olympic years.

It took some time before the Event settled on what to call itself, and indeed over the years it has continued to be modified. In 1949 it launched as BADMINTON 3 DAYS EVENT. In the public's mind the shuttlecock game sprung to mind. To help a bit in 1951 the name changed to The British Horse Society OLYMPIC HORSE TRIALS at BADMINTON. With the

LITTLE BOOK OF **BADMINTON**

sport of Eventing also known as Horse Trials, this created a different confusion, as these Horse Trials were 'trials' for the Olympics, NOT the Horse Trials AT the Olympics, which would also be referred to as the Olympic Horse Trials! In 1956 it became The British Horse Society BADMINTON HORSE TRIALS and by 1970 was simply BADMINTON HORSE TRIALS. It then appended 'For the Whitbread Trophy'. Next it was WHITBREAD CHAMPIONSHIPS BADMINTON, then THE Whitbread Championships Badminton. The brewers, Whitbread, began a long (31-year) sponsorship in a modest way in 1961 and were happy for the Event to go unbranded for some years afterwards. When Mitsubishi took over sponsoring in 1992 it became The Badminton Horse Trials for the Mitsubishi Motors Trophy. Then it slipped its date into the title The 1997 Mitsubishi Motors Badminton Horse Trials. That became The Mitsubishi Motors Badminton Horse Trials; BADMINTON HORSE TRIALS MITSUBISHI MOTORS, and finally Mitsubishi Motors Badminton Horse Trials 2013. In the early Sixties the Event had two other titles, explained below.

No longer, however, is there confusion with the shuttlecocks. Badminton with a capital 'B' can mean only one thing.

The Event had become an established fixture in the sporting calendar in its first 10 years of existence, not just as a public spectacle, but also as an ambition for aspiring horsemen (of both sexes) from around the world. It had also had its sabbatical year at Windsor in 1955. Badminton became the ultimate equestrian challenge, where riders were competing as much against what the course designer had erected for them as against fellow competitors.

By 1958, with fairly rudimentary qualifications, the number of entries was getting potentially unmanageable. Even with tighter requirements in 1959 there were 100 entries (though then, as now, not all would come to post). The main problem was how to judge that many Dressage tests in one day. (Neither the Duke, nor the organisers wanted an extra Dressage day at that time). The solution, not entirely popular, was to split the entry into two sections of those with the most qualifying points and those with fewer. The severity of the competition was the same for both classes: same Dressage test (but separate

Far Left: *Roads and Tracks*

CHANGES

panel of judges), same Endurance day and same final Show Jumping course. The sections were called The Great Badminton Championship Event and The Little Badminton Event. The titles came from the two Badminton villages, but the term 'Little' was unfortunate. It didn't really solve the problem, because in the end both sections ended up being small with the largest aggregate being 59 competitors. After six years Badminton returned to being the one big senior section that everyone wanted to win, and eventually two full days of Dressage became accepted. The optimum number of starters is now about 80, from an entry of near 150.

The basic layout changed when the Dressage and jumping moved to an arena to the north west of the front of the house and grandstand seats were erected, and it was around this arena that the tented village of trade stands began to grow. The Cross Country had several different routes until it settled for many years with the 'Ten minute box' where horses and riders would have a break after the Roads and Tracks and Steeplechase phases, just to the west of the Lake. On some of the early courses the Lake

was the final obstacle. Traditionally the course would alternate in direction either setting off left in front of the house or right towards Huntsman's Close. The Steeplechase moved from the Beaufort Point to Point course to the Slaits outside the Deer Park, where the coach park and air strip are situated. The chase course was an oval, then became a figure of eight.

Several years ago the start and finish moved into the main arena, with the first and last jumps in front of the grandstands.

The Event had always been run in April, initially to fit in with the Estate Office policy. This did have a couple of disadvantages. It was a bit early in the year to attract a large international field, especially as the big Championships had settled into a late autumn timescale. It was also pretty early in what was becoming a regular, and full, spring season of domestic events. Badminton horses didn't get much of a warm up.

British spring weather had also done its worst, causing the Event to be cancelled in 1966 and 1975 and being reduced to a One Day Event in 1963. There were other years when it ran, but in horrible conditions for competitors, and more importantly, the spectators.

In the cancelled years the horses and riders could probably have coped, but the grounds would not have been able to take all the vehicles.

When Badminton was rained off for the third time in 1987, it was eventually decided to shift the date to early May, where it remains.

The horse trot ups in front of the judges and veterinary panel used to be held in the quadrangle of the magnificent stable yard. However, over the years they had become very much a public spectacle. This was all to the good, as it showed the world how open the sport was about animal welfare. The stable yard started to overflow for these inspections, so from the early 1980s they moved to the front of the house, where wagons are towed into place to act as temporary grandstands.

The rules of the sport change in small ways almost yearly, but one difference from the old days of death and glory, when it was expected of a rider to scoop themselves up after a fearsome fall and carry on, is that now fallers are obliged to retire. The relative importance of the phases has also shifted a bit. The emphasis is as ever on the Cross Country, but good weather on that day can make the Dressage over influential. The Jumping phase used to be very expensive, with 10 penalties for one pole down. This was reduced to five, and is now a mere four, in line with pure Show Jumping.

The inspiration, host and instigator of the Badminton Horse Trials, the 10th Duke of Beaufort, died in 1984 and was succeeded by his cousin David Somerset, who had lived in The Cottage and former Dower House, by the Kennels, for many years, and had been on the organising committee of the Horse Trials.

There was never a doubt that the new Duke would be an equally enthusiastic host as his forebear. He, himself, had ridden at Badminton on several occasions and had been a close runner-up with Countryman III to Sheila Waddington in 1959.

Over the years the sport had again become increasingly broadly based, despite the UK remaining easily the country with the most events, the International Equestrian Federation, the FEI, was trying to get more countries to compete at international level, not least to keep the International Olympic Committee happy to retain horses in the Games. There were perennial concerns about the limited international participation and the expense and inconvenience of running a competition that needs such an enormous amount of land to take place, and within reason as close as possible to the host city.

The space problem was also a disadvantage to emerging equestrian nations. There had been moves and test events, after the millennium, to abolish the Endurance phases of Roads and Tracks and Steeplechase. At a stroke this would completely alter the complexity of the competition and remove it once and for all from its historic military roots, where long distance fitness and mount conserving horsemanship were the essence of the test. The purists were outraged. The fact remained, however, that for years the Endurance phase had been

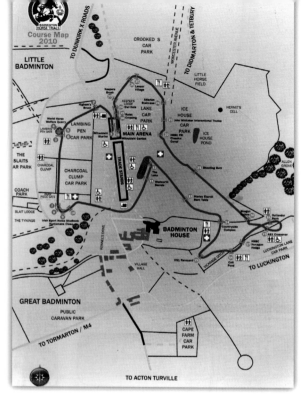

Above: *Short format map*

gone 'short format' by 2005, and though Badminton held out for as long as possible, there seemed little logic in running an event that wasn't in effect the same sport as the European, World and Olympic competitions.

2006 was the start of the new era, though it is doubtful that any more than an informed handful of the now vast crowds would have noticed the difference, or really cared. The Endurance phase was not part of their day out, was not televised and in reality no longer missed.

In equestrian terms there was a lot of debate as to whether, rather heavier, Dressage specialist type horses would now become the norm, and whether riders would get their horses fit enough. In the early days of short format this was a concern, but after a few years, trainers, riders and selectors were starting to settle down to a consensus.

The standard day format for Badminton was: Riders briefing and course open for walking, followed by first horse inspection in the evening, Wednesday; two days of Dressage, Thursday and Friday; Cross Country, Saturday; final horse inspection and Show Jumping, Sunday. This was

getting shorter and shorter, and even Badminton's Cross Country course, which used to venture out of the park over the Luckington Lane, had been shortened from a 15-minute, 35-fence marathon to just over 11 minutes and 28 numbered obstacles.

All the major championships had

changed once in the Seventies, when the crowds had become so big that it was decided for one year to run the Cross Country on the Friday. What really worked, however, was a revised traffic and parking plan and it returned swiftly to the big box office Saturday the following year.

There can be things beyond the control of the best organisers and sometimes a balance needs to be achieved. Unintended consequences can dictate many things. For the 2010 season the BBC had won back Formula One motor racing from ITV and the producers told Badminton that they could not guarantee Sunday coverage of the Cross Country highlights and the finale if the Event clashed with a car race. Since The Badminton date was the May Bank Holiday, it was suggested the Trials run the Cross Country on the Sunday and finish on Bank Holiday Monday. It was difficult for everyone to get their heads round, but it did work to a certain extent. Indeed the gates for the Dressage/ shopping days were better on Friday/ Saturday than Thursday/ Friday. It ran like this, through the cancelled year of 2012, until the BBC lost out to SKY Sports for the motor racing. Saturday

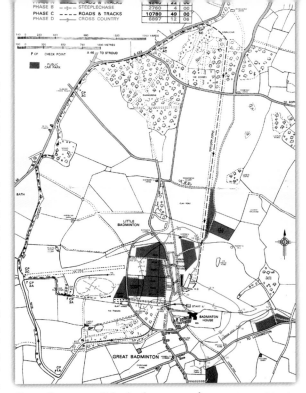

Above: *What the distance used to be*

Cross Country will be back to normal, a week forward, in 2014.

One of the reasons that a sporting event that has a very identifiable history has survived and continues to grow is that it has kept on evolving in a more welfare-based, less military and far more media-exposed environment.

Dramas

With an event as big as Badminton which has been running for over 50 years there have, of course, been incidents, some tragic, some sportingly disastrous, some frustrating and some comical.

As early as the third Badminton in 1951, when the Event was anything but established, the weather in the build-up had been atrocious. Trevor Horn had designed his course, duly built by the head forester, Mr. Chappell. The first entry of international riders had arrived, ready to take on the British and Irish. The course had to be changed three times before Cross Country day, with rails being secured the night before. The Event was nothing on the scale it is today, but it could have been a fatal blow to have had to cancel in only its third year.

As Badminton became more famous and the infrastructure more involved, with the public gate now substantial, cancellation would have serious financial repercussions. In 1959 with another dreadful April weekend for the Trials, five jumps were removed from the Cross Country course and another four were lowered to ensure safe passage.

Longer term forethought was employed in 1963, which had one of the worst springs on record. Organisers decided to reduce the competition to a One Day Event, the format for the

network of warm up events that had sprung up around the country. This meant no Endurance phase of Roads and Tracks and Steeplechase with the Cross Country the final phase. At least the Event took place. This one-off was won by Susan Fleet and The Gladiator, though the whole event has been removed from the Badminton records and categorised 'cancelled' as it wasn't considered a true Three Day Event.

Oddly the Badminton of 1955, which was actually held at Windsor, does count as a true Badminton record. This is perhaps due to the fact that it was won by the future autocratic Badminton Director, Frank Weldon, who may have arbitrated the inclusion!

In 1966, with many trade stands in situ and riders and horses converging on the Gloucestershire park, the incessant and continuing rain of the previous week defeated the organisers for the first time, and the Event was cancelled the day before the riders' briefing. To keep spirits up the traditional cocktail party in Badminton House went ahead for those who had arrived anyway.

Again the spring of 1975 had been unduly wet, but it was thought to be worth the risk to carry on. Both days of Dressage took place in a deluge, with horses squelching through their tests, and making a thorough bog of the arena. A full complement of riders and officials went to the Thursday cocktail party, but there was a scent of defeatism as the rain continued to pour. Sure enough at close of play on Friday evening the inevitable cancellation took place.

The course was again probably rideable, but the park would not be able to cope with the thousands of cars and tramping feet. It was a bitter disappointment to all concerned, especially for the riders, who had actually started the competition.

Over the years much of the park used for the Event had had substantial ground work done, with drainage and hard core turfed over on the road edges, and also on the take-offs and landings at the jumps. Despite this the rain did

its worst again in 1987 and the Event was pulled in advance. This was the nudge that persuaded the Estate and organisers to have a rethink and move the competition from April to early May. This move was popular with the riders, especially the international fraternity, as it put Badminton at a more suitable time in the spring calendar. It was hoped the move would also appease the weather gods.

Not so. In the build-up year to the London Olympics in 2012, Badminton was looking forward to celebrating its link to the 1948 London Games, which lit the torch for Badminton to exist in the first place. Again it had been a spring of incessant rain, but now with no Endurance phase, a shorter Cross Country than in the past and a pretty robust infrastructure, organisers kept their nerve until the very last minute, only to have to admit defeat on the Monday of the Event, when half the course was submerged in water.

The cry often goes out in a cancellation year: 'Why not reschedule?' But there are so many aspects that are tied in. TV scheduling, tent hire, competition calendar, hotel bookings and road closures all go to make another later date impossible.

It wasn't the wet that put paid to the 2001 Event. There was an outbreak of foot and mouth disease which decimated the country's livestock, and led to distressing news footage of burning pyres of farm animals. Though the prep work for each following Badminton starts pretty well the minute the previous one is over, it was obvious early on that it wouldn't be running that year, so the expense of setting up was avoided. Its loss, however, still left a big hole in the sporting calendar.

Ironically it was an unusually warm spring that had an effect on Badminton 2007. The weather forecast had promised a good few days of rain in the run-up to the Event, so it was thought unnecessary to water the Cross Country track, as is often done at race courses. The groundsman's dilemma is that a watered course, which is subsequently rained on, can become very sticky. Badminton remained unwatered but the rain never came.

When the riders first got to have a look at the course and noticed cracks in the ground they expressed their concern in no uncertain way. Many, including the reigning World and European Champion, Zara Phillips, on her Badminton debut, decided to just go through the motions of their Dressage tests and then withdrew.

There was a serious threat of a full scale rider revolt. Frantic efforts were made overnight to lay a dirt track on the turf, which succeeded in taking some of the sting out of the ground. Those who were prepared to have a go, found that all the effort had made the track just about acceptable, but the public relations damage had been done.

As so often happens, if luck is going against you, other things go wrong, as they did for the Badminton team that year. A French horse had a freak accident on the course and died after staking itself on a broken flag post on one of the jumps. These wooden posts had been used without incident all round the world since the beginning of time. Now they are all made of flexible plastic.

Badminton Cross Country had always been televised live, with the inbuilt risk that a hold up on the course would coincide with transmission. 2007 was the experienced producer's first year as number one in charge. He was just about to go on air with no action

to show. Presenter, Clare Balding, on 'talkback' said to him, 'Gerry, there is nothing happening, I haven't a clue what I'm going to say.' Gerry's reply: 'We'll soon find out...cue Clare!'. She did a brilliant job of filling until the competition restarted. Now the Cross Country phase only goes live to digital viewers, who, by definition, are Eventing knowledgeable, and

would understand a break. The 'real' programme is recorded, edited overnight and presented as a package.

Immediately after that Event a massive investment was made in turf management to ensure that a similar going problem is unlikely to occur again. The only possible downside to this is that the route of the track, in whichever way round it goes, will

probably never again reach out to some further parts of the park.

The Badminton course has always lived up to its reputation as the pinnacle test of Cross Country skill and bravery, and in the earlier years nobody minded if there was a certain amount of attrition, with perhaps at least one-third of the combinations failing to get round. Apart from one or two statistically easier years, this was the average until 1973 when just

43% made it round. But that didn't tell half the story. A good third of the field never made past the third fence. Described as 'The Coffin' it was a familiar type of jump, with a post and rail down a drop to a ditch, a slope up and a post and rail out. It may have been higher than in former incarnations, the slope might have been steeper, and the distances between the elements might have been tighter. It may also have been that this tricky fence was so early on the course.

The spectators expect a few thrills and spills, but with so many horses not even getting to fence four, the paying public rightly felt very short changed that year, and many riders commented that their honest horses had been overfaced.

There have been some hard luck stories and some great escapes. Mark Phillips, riding arguably his best, but fated horse, Persian Holiday, was negotiating Huntsman's Close when his rein broke and had to retire.

In 1986 British rider, and for the equestrian media, upcoming star, Polly Schwerdt, was riding her tiny horse, Dylan II, who was attempting to become the first horse to complete the Event five times in a row. After clearing the first fence they glanced off a moving vehicle which had strayed onto the course. Polly got off to see if any damage had been done, which luckily it hadn't, but her concentration had gone, and they had a refusal at the next fence. They completed, but her

dismount added to her time and the 20 jumping penalties dropped her to fourteenth place.

New Zealand rider, Vaughn Jefferis, had a technical nightmare in 1990. He was having a great ride on Enterprise, but early on in his round his helmet chinstrap came undone. Safety rules dictated that he should have stopped and done it up. No doubt the adrenalin was flowing and he carried on blissfully until he was flagged down by an official near the end of the course, and summarily eliminated.

In 1999 Australian rider, Stuart Tinney, had jumped through the Lake complex with Tex, but as they emerged from the water, the horse locked onto a sight line which must have seemed like a gap in the crowd. This was because the spectators were on a lower level to the others, as this was the disabled viewing pen. Tex took hold of the bit, leaped the spectator fence and knocked over US cameraman, Melvin Cox, who was back the next day, strapped up. Luckily no wheelchairs were up-ended.

Many a Badminton has been lost at the last minute, when the overnight leader has a fence down, but one of the most awful jumping disasters happened to a protégé of Mark Phillips, Claire Bowley. She had been Young Rider National Champion and led the Dressage at her first Badminton attempt in 1990 with Fair Share. By the end of the Cross Country day she was still in the lead by a narrow margin of one and a half points. Sadly Claire got stage fright and the horse bashed down five poles, incurred time penalties and dropped to twelfth.

Back in 1979, US rider, Karen Sachey, in line for a prize, was eliminated at the final Show Jumping fence when High Kite refused three times.

In 1995, for the only time, the overnight leader after the Cross Country, Chaka, ridden by William Fox-Pitt, was failed at the final trot up.

The unexpected and sad coda to the 1976 Event was, as noted in the section on multiple winners, Lucinda Prior-Palmer's champion, Wideawake, dropping down dead in the prize giving.

On the course in 1973 Rachel Bayliss and Gurgle the Greek had managed to negotiate the infamous 'Coffin', but at the far end of the course was a jump called The Stockholm Fence, a huge log slung high over a ditch, approached down a slope. Gurgle slid to a stop, which would normally incur 20 penalties for a refusal. By this stage Rachel and Gurgle were under the log, but having, within the rules, passed between the jump's flags, kept going and clambered out the other side with a clean sheet! Not only were the rules changed after this, but modern fence construction would make that stunt impossible today.

One of the unforgettable feats of horsemanship seen at Badminton was in 1995 when Mark was riding Bertie Blunt. At the Vicarage Pond, only about a quarter way round the course, Mark's left stirrup broke. He rode the rest of the way with just his right foot secured and ended the day in fifth position. That year five horses failed the final inspection, an unusually high number, and Bertie Blunt was amongst them. The heroics of the day before were to no avail.

Over the years the Event has coped with streakers, bomb scares created by rogue remote cameras, wash outs, dry outs, rule changers and all the emotions from elation to devastation. It is one of the reasons that it is never predictable.

Far Left: *Mark Todd riding without a pedal*

International Winners

Far Right: *Bruce Davidson on Eagle Lion*

In over 60 years of Badminton there have been only 12 winners riding under a foreign flag, despite the Event becoming truly International in only its third year, 1951. Two of these were in the first four years.

As described in the section on the early years, at that third Event, the Swiss, whose horses had spent the winter stabled and exercised in indoor schools, sent seven riders with eight horses. All but one completed.

By and large the Swiss were way ahead of the other nations in the Dressage, which was to be expected, but proving the point that a well trained horse would 'obey' the rider, their mounts duly obeyed the instructions to jump the unfamiliar Cross Country obstacles. It certainly showed considerable mutual trust between horse and rider, which is as much of the point of the sport as sheer bravado.

Also somewhat surprisingly that year, when the going was muddy and testing, the somewhat overweight and under bred horses from the Cantons coped well enough for speed. Of the 21 finishers only three had clean Show Jumping rounds, including the runner-up for GB, Jane Drummond-Hay and Happy Knight, but the overnight leader had enough in hand to have one down for 10 penalties. Capt. Hans Schwarzenbach and Vae Victis finished with a margin of 19 points and became the only continental competitors to win Badminton until 2008.

The following year, in 1952, the Event only attracted entries from Britain and Ireland, as it had done in the first two runnings. This was the Olympic year for which Badminton had initially been inaugurated, and most spectators were interested to see how the British contenders would do. However, an amateur Irish rider from the army, Mark Darley, and his small flighty mare, Emily Little, the latter a thoroughbred descended from the Darley Arabian, and the former from the very Darley family to have introduced the blood line, upset the form book.

It was a stiff Cross Country, with eight new fences, that caused considerable trouble. Only 15 of the 26 entries completed the Event. Darley's margin was only two points from Brian Young and Dandy, whose 20.25 Show Jumping penalties handed the Irishman the prize.

It was the build-up to the Rome Olympics of 1960 that saw a supreme feat of training by the Australian squad. They had come seven-handed to Badminton in 1956 prior to the Games. Ironically the Olympics were in Melbourne, but the Australian quarantine laws were so strict that the equestrian competitions were deputised to Stockholm. Australia was just out of the medals there.

The Rome squad came to Europe by ship, leaving six months before the Games, and taking five weeks to travel. Their freighter was carrying wool, which had to be delivered first to Italy. The Australians laid a riding surface on deck to keep their horses fit.

Bill Roycroft, on the 15hh former polo pony, Our Solo, and his countryman, Laurie Morgan and Salad Days, were in second and third after the Cross Country, but the overnight leader, Anneli Drummond-Hay, had two show jumps down to drop to third, giving the Australians a one two. Three other Australians were in the top twelve which gave them a great run before Rome.

There, Roycroft had a heavy fall and Our Solo went back to the, luckily nearby, stables. The horse was caught and brought back, and the concussed Roycroft was put back in the saddle and completed the course. With one Australian eliminated, three riders had to continue on the final day to produce a team score. Bill was discharged from hospital, pumped with painkillers, duly show-jumped clear and helped Australia

Far Left: *Bill Roycroft on Stoney Crossing*

Right: *Andrew Hoy on Moonfleet*

to a sensational team gold medal. The individual gold went to Laurie Morgan and Salad Days.

Back at Badminton in 1961, Laurie Morgan and Salad Days were overnight leaders after the Cross Country. He was a bit lucky to be there as he had gone wrong twice in his Dressage test and Salad Days had got straddled over two of the Cross Country obstacles. Laurie stayed in the saddle and strongly urged his horse to extricate itself both times. He didn't have a fence in hand in the Jumping. The pair went painfully slowly but cleanly, and did incur .75 of a time penalty. The caution paid off, however, as Morgan made it two Badmintons in two years for Australia.

1965 saw the last of the 1949 pioneers entered at Badminton. At that first Event Ireland's Lt. Eddie Boylan came tenth with Cool Star. He returned again in 1960 with Corrigneagh to come fifteenth, having been promoted to Major in the intervening years. His latest entry was Durlas Eile and they had a narrow lead in the Dressage over Sheila Waddington and Glenamoy, which they maintained after the Cross Country.

Glenamoy faulted in the Show Jumping to let Bill Roycroft, who went clear with Eldorado, up into second spot. Durlas Eile had one fence down and a foot in the water jump to earn 20 penalties, but still held on to win by 7.2.

It would be another 15 years before a foreign rider would win Badminton again. That was the unheralded Mark Todd from New Zealand, who took the title on Southern Comfort in 1980. Mark remains the only non-British rider to have won Badminton more than once, as is recorded in the section on Badminton's finest.

Bruce Davidson, the best Three Day Eventer the USA has produced, had based himself in Britain in the spring of 1974 to make a concerted attempt on the title. There was a discrepancy of 10 seconds between the optimum time given to the competitors and that given to the time keepers. Bruce, ever the perfectionist, thought he had made it inside the time by a calculated whisker. The time keepers had him slow, and he was given 13.6 time penalties. His appeal wasn't successful, and though he wouldn't have won it, since the Champions, Mark Phillips and Columbus finished on their

Dressage score, Bruce and Irish Cap missed runner-up spot to come third. His compensation was to become World Champion that autumn at Burghley. He retained the title four years later at Lexington with Might Tango.

Bruce came second in 1982 with JJ Babu and fourth with Eagle Lion in 1994. In 1995 his campaign started well, as he and Eagle Lion were in third place after the Dressage. For the good combinations the course rode quite easily that year, so the leading Dressage three were in the same spot after Cross Country. On top was William Fox-Pitt with Chaka, and in second, the reigning Olympic champion, Matt Ryan, with Kibah Tic Toc.

Chaka failed the final horse inspection, and last to go, Matt, had one fence down and half a time fault to drop to third. At last Bruce had won Badminton.

Rather as with the Australians in the early Sixties, the USA was going through a good run in the mid-Nineties. Two years after Bruce Davidson's victory a record 42 combinations jumped the Cross Country course without jumping penalties, 16 without time penalties. For the second year running Ian Stark and Stanwick Ghost led after the first two days. In 1996 two jumps down dropped him to sixth and promoted David O'Connor of the USA to third place.

Mary King in second after Cross Country in 1997 had one down to promote David O'Connor to second. Ian and Stanwick Ghost entered the arena last to go and knocked no fewer than five down to drop out of all prizes. David, with Custom Made became the second American to win Badminton in three years.

It was to be another 11 years before another non–British rider was to take the winner's trophy. Southern hemisphere riders have put up a consistently good performance since the Roycroft and Morgan days. As well as Mark Todd, New Zealand's former world champion, Blyth Tait, came second three times, from the same country Vaughn Jefferis has been runner-up, as has Andrew Nicholson.

Multiple Australian Olympian, Andrew Hoy, had had some chances since his first appearance in 1979, but it wasn't until 2006 that it all came together when he gave owner, Sue Magnier, an unforgettable weekend with Moonfleet adding Badminton to her Two Thousand Guineas triumph with George Washington.

The next year, when several top combinations withdrew because of hard going on the course, British born, but Australian by marriage, Lucinda Fredericks, took her chance to put her name on the trophy with Headley Britannia.

In 2008, for the first time since 1951, a combination from continental Europe, Nicolas Touzaint and Hildago de L'Ile for France, won in front of a euphoric travelling fan club waving their tricolours.

Joining the Antipodean roll of honour in 2010 was the relatively unheralded combination of British-based Australian, Paul Tapner and Inonothing. Paul was lucky to be there because his horse had been injured at the World Equestrian Games the previous September, but they had posted some winning runs before Badminton, and the rider was quietly confident. His blistering Cross Country, recorded on head cam, set him up to join the roll of honour.

The Event now has entries from a truly international cross section, but it is the southern hemisphere riders who have relieved the hosts most frequently of the ultimate prize in Eventing.

Famous Jumps

What has made Badminton famous over its 60-year history is its daunting Cross Country course. Though the emphasis has changed over the years on what is considered difficult, the Badminton challenge has always been the greatest in the sport.

If in the very early incarnations it resembled a very varied hunting run, it has progressed through the frankly terrifying era, to the very complicated brain teasing, pinpoint aiming test of more recent years.

Since the Endurance phases of Roads and Tracks went in 2006, the horses now start the Cross Country fresh, without having already gone 10 miles, but today the obstacles tend to be in tight clusters.

This is partly for television purposes, partly for the crowd to see pockets of action, but also indicative of the direction in which the sport is progressing. There is more strain, both mental and physical, in this continual direction changing. In the early days of Short Format some horses were finishing MORE tired than before. Some suspected this was because they hadn't been as prepared as they would have been for the long distance version, but it was more probably because a busier, shorter test was indeed more tiring.

The course is never the same year on year, but several natural features of the park have provided permanent sites for the course designers to weave their

magic. Some jumps were introduced as a brand new challenge, some adapted to Badminton's terrain from other international competitions. Several of these obstacles achieved mythical status, often because in their year of introduction they were thought either unjumpable or very frightening. These, like Becher's Brook on the Grand National course, became the ones for riders to bore their grandchildren with. The trick of the course designer was to make the jumps much more simple for the horses than they seemed to the riders, and also to provide a real 'OOH ' factor for the crowds, many of whom may have jumped modest things out hunting, but marvelled at the heroics of the Badminton few.

The Badminton terrain is pretty flat, but there are two long ditches, one separating the deer park to farm land, the other a long drainage channel known as the Vicarage Ditch. For many years the course actually crossed a real country road, the Luckington Lane. Right in

front of the house is a large manmade lake, and heading north, the only bit of undulating ground. To the west is an old stoneworks and then heading back south a wooded copse, Huntsman's Close.

Over the years the course has been designed by Trevor Horn, with The Duke of Beaufort and Brigadier Bowden-Smith, partly by Colonel 'Babe' Moseley, Colonel Cox-Cox, Colonel Frank Weldon and for over 20 years by Hugh Thomas. Surprisingly the actual permitted dimensions of the

jumps for competitions at this level haven't changed in the main since the 1912 Olympics.

From the inaugural Event there was an Irish Bank, initially with a cinder covering, memorably jumped in one by the reigning champion, Golden Willow, the second year. It was subsequently turfed over and is still part of the course today. For some years it has had an obstacle on top of it and various options on landing.

The Lake, undoubtedly the crowd favourite, has also played a part from the beginning with many variations. There have been many duckings over the years, but spectacular as they are, most have provided a soft, if wet landing. The water used to be much deeper than is now permitted, but the jumps there have included a simple log in, a big single rail with a drop; a double of rails and drop with an up and out second part; a drop into the Lake, a hung log jump, actually in the middle, and a boat house out; a jump in followed by an on and off jetty, and an out option and some woven willow waves followed by some narrow brushes in the water.

The Quarry once had a stone wall with a steep drop after, and out up a bank double step. When one year an out of control horse jumped the drop wall going uphill, what seemed impossible was incorporated as a real jump by Frank Weldon the following year. The contours have softened recently to present some large logs on undulating slopes.

The Normandy Bank was once THE iconic Badminton jump, used going in both directions, either just before or just after the Lake in the 1970s and 80s. It was an upright bank with no real room for a stride on top (though some did put one in) a post and rail and enormous drop on landing. This was a Weldon copy of a jump at Haras du Pin, though considerably more spectacular than the original.

The Ski Jump was either the one before or one after the Normandy Bank, so there were three major challenges in a row, whichever way round the course was running. This was a smallish log at the top of a very steep slope and then an upright obstacle at the bottom.

The Horsens Bridge was another of Weldon's imports which was placed as an entry or exit to the deer park over the ditch. Again it had a now unfashionable drop on landing, but it produced some extravagant leaps, with little trouble,

and was another one which left the spectators in awe.

The Luckington Lane jumps were two large, natural hedges, in and out, over the road, which had to be taken at quite an acute angle. This took riders to the farm of estate tenant, Tom Smith.

Tom Smith's Walls were two stone

Above: *The Ski Jump*

Far Left: *The Quarry*

walls at right angles, joined at the corner. The 'easy' route was to jump the first element and take a sharp turn to the next part. However, the brave could opt to save a lot of precious time and jump the right angle corner in one. Those who did earned great crowd respect.

At the Vicarage V similar options presented themselves. Along the main ditch stood an upright post and rail. There is another drainage ditch at 90 degrees. The slower route would be ditch, turn, rail over ditch. The brave would line it up, cut the angle, and jump both elements in one.

The Hexagon Hedges is Hugh Thomas's unique take on the same site, with a series of very narrow brush jumps over the Vicarage Ditch.

The Carisma Pond is another Thomas innovation, where he widened the ditch where the old Open Water used to be, to give him many options at a second water splash on the course.

The Whitbread Drays was a favourite in the days of the former sponsor, when competitors actually jumped two real beer drays. The modern equivalent is jumping the back of two Mitsubishi Pick Up trucks,

nowadays usually positioned as part of the Lake jump complex.

Some fences have been clever crowd pleasers which look spectacular from the landing side, with a gaping ditch, but in reality, on take-off the fence is easy, and the horses naturally 'carry' over the optical illusion drop and land on almost level ground. A good example of this was the Pardubice Taxis, a brush, in or out of the deer park, sometimes as early as fence three. It was inspired by Czechoslovakia's answer to Becher's Brook. It was built in honour of Badminton rider, Chris Collins, who won the Czech Grand National.

Every year riders and spectators wait to see what ingenious new challenges have sprouted out of the Badminton turf since their last visit.

Media at Badminton

Far Right: *Former Press Officer Jim Gilmore keeps the 70s' press pack under control*

As Badminton promoted itself from the very start as something out of the ordinary in the horse world, it was always going to be picked up by the broadsheet press. This was an era when hunting was reported in the media, so an equestrian competition that involved many attributes associated with the chase, was bound to be of interest.

When the Queen came for the first time in 1952, and watched the Event in great informality, the Event received a boost with picture specials in the illustrated magazines.

By 1954, on only its sixth running, Badminton had become sufficiently established for the BBC to send an outside broadcast team for the first of an unbroken run of TV coverage.

By 1969 there was sufficient press interest both nationally, but also with a vibrant local press, that Gloucestershire newspaperman, Jim Gilmore, suggested to the then Director, Frank Weldon, that it might be a good idea to have a press tent. Weldon agreed that this was a good idea and promptly asked Jim to become Badminton's first Press Officer, a role he held for over 30 years. The first press tent was a modest affair, but a media operation was very timely as within a couple of years, interest in Badminton from the press went into orbit with the arrival of Princess Anne as a competitor.

Badminton Horse Trials was on the front pages as well as the sports sections.

Mark Phillips went on to win the Event on the Queen's horse, Columbus, to cement public interest. Jim Gilmore was in his element, running a war of attrition with the paparazzi who found it hard to respect the Princess as a regular competitor.

The Princess Anne effect had put Badminton into another PR league and though there was a bit of a dip after she stopped competing, there were always other Royals or celebrities who found their pictures in the papers, magazines

The interest in the sport was ramped up further when the Princess started her involvement with the dashing, uniformed, young Army officer, who had won Badminton.

and Sunday supplements. The whole mass media circus kicked off again when Zara Phillips, who had become both World and European Three Day Eventing Champion without having yet ridden at Badminton, first entered in 2007. Sadly that was the year that the going on the Cross Country was questionable and Zara was one of the high profile riders to withdraw after the Dressage. It would have been a serious PR glitch even without a Champion 'Royal' deciding not to risk her top horse. There was a considerable repair job for the organisation and media team to put right for the following year.

The 1970s was a Golden era for horses on television, when The Horse of

Above: *The state of the art Media Centre*

the Year Show was Broadcast primetime on the five days of its run. A Badminton winner would be part of the sports section on the BBC News.

There is no doubt that the public perception of the sport was (and still to an extent is) a very up market set-up. It was surprisingly followed by a very broad fan base, perhaps like TV series such as the contemporary *Upstairs Downstairs* and today's *Downton Abbey*.

Seeing a Princess risking an ignominious ducking was very democratic. Add to that mix a genuine sporting superstar in the six times winning, Viceroy's granddaughter, Lucinda Prior-Palmer, a Stately Home and the dulcet commentary of the patrician, Dorian Williams, and Raymond Brooks-Ward, and the BBC had a great package.

At the start there was only really *Horse & Hound* magazine as a specialist outlet, though the other glossy up market publications like *Country Life* and *The Field* would cover the Trials. Now there are many specialist equestrian titles, all of which feature the Event.

Local media has also grown, with regional papers and magazines following the fortunes of Badminton riders from their areas.

The small press tent of the early days began to get bigger, and when Mitsubishi took over the sponsorship in 1992 they invested a lot of money into a state of the art Media Centre.

The media world has changed out of all recognition from the days when four or five national papers sent writers and the local Gloucestershire press sent representatives. Badminton is now such a sporting phenomenon that many of the Dailies send feature writers.

The press office send out about three releases in the build-up to the Trials, usually one in the New Year to alert the world that it is all systems go for May, then one which discusses the entries that year in mid-March, on the day that the list is published and finally one to coincide with an invitation-only press day when journalists get to drive round the course in the sponsor's demonstration vehicles after coffee in the Great Hall, where the shuttlecock game originated. Everyone then has lunch hosted by the Duke of Beaufort in Badminton House. Other releases will go out if there is a specific bit of news such as a renewal of a TV contract.

Though the BBC still do the main broadcast, some foreign countries take

Left: *Raymond Brooks-Ward*

the feed, and highlights go out on platforms such as Eurosport and Sky. There are also one or two documentary crews each time, and in an Olympic year there have been as many as 13 film crews on site, which the media team have to service.

For many years the BBC paid rights to come and make the TV programme, but in recent years Badminton Horse Trials effectively make the programme themselves and sell it to the BBC, who guarantee to broadcast it if it follows certain guidelines. In reality the people who actually make the programme are the same former BBC team who now make it as freelancers.

There have been two or three full length documentaries over the years, where the producers have put all their eggs in one basket and decided to do a 'quest to Badminton' programme. In 1962 sponsors, Whitbread, made a film following Anneli Drummond-Hay and her horse, Merely-a-Monarch, in their build-up and during the competition.

They struck gold as the combination won by the biggest ever margin. In 1979, however, a team making 'The Great Event' didn't want to take such a risk, and covered all bases by following two top riders, Jane Holderness-Roddam and Chris Collins. They both had two horses. Not one of the four horses completed the three days! In 2012 both a Chinese and French crew were to make hour-long programmes, only for the Event to be cancelled at the very last minute, because of the waterlogged course.

Sometimes another show, such as a pre-General Election politics programme will choose to broadcast live from the Trials. These all take meticulous planning.

Badminton now has its own localised 'Badminton Radio' throughout the Event, which does interviews with riders, gives traffic bulletins, gives some commentary and advertises the trade stands. There is also a team that syndicates radio interviews to local stations.

Into all this traditional media have

arrived the more recent platforms. A sizeable amount of journalism is now online, and the Media Centre will accommodate some equestrian websites, but has to screen out those which are not much more than glorified personal notice boards. Badminton has a very successful website of its own www.badminton-horse.co.uk which has everything from online booking, places to stay, results service, up to date stories, video interviews, history, previous winners, photo albums and associated links. Nearer the Event there is a virtual 'walk' round the Cross Country course and also a filmed walk with a past rider, explaining the intricacies of the track.

The Trials also have a phone app, where all information can be accessed on site during the Event. Badminton has a Facebook page and its own Twitter account @bhorsetrials. There is also footage on YouTube and members of the media team service this new media. It has all come a long way from that first tent in 1969, The Media Centre now accredits nearly 500 journalists, photographers, web meisters and film crews, on top of the team that makes the main TV programme for the BBC.

Behind the Scenes

Far Right: Frank Weldon with the 11th Duke

A once a year event the size of Badminton has a whole structure of organisation, which comes together for the one crucial week. There is a small nucleus of five which works full time for the Trials, which grows sharply after the New Year. When the Trials are in full swing this multiplies a hundred times, with a great many volunteers coming year after year.

At the helm is the Director of the Event. In over 60 years Badminton has had less than a handful. Uniquely to Badminton the Director has been the course designer. Trevor Horn's first course in 1949 started just below the stables, went over the Luckington Lane and back, and finished heading north up Worcester Avenue. Horn handed over the reins to his brother-in-law, Colonel Gordon Cox-Cox in 1954, whose course that year was one of the biggest yet seen. After the Event of 1964, Britain suffered a second disappointing Olympics at Tokyo, and the gold at Stockholm in 1956 was the only prize to show for the original concept of Badminton as a springboard for British success.

At the suggestion of the Duke's heir, Mr. David Somerset, former winner Col. Frank Weldon, who had already contributed fence design ideas, was drafted in as course designer in 1965. This was to herald a Golden age, though stalled by the cancellation of the 1966 Event. His 1966 course which was

completely new apart from one fence from 1965, was used in 1967.

That year Weldon took over as Director and returned the Event to a single section competition, to general approval. The Event now had enjoyed sponsorship from brewers, Whitbread, since 1966, and this helped with the financial security of the operation, but Frank was a designing genius. It was his ability to build seemingly impossible obstacles, through endless observation of horses jumping, 'to know exactly what a horse can do.' It was he who perfected the type of fence that would terrify the riders, seriously impress the spectators and generally be well within the horses' scope. Much of this effect was achieved by jumps with massive drops on the landing side, or sometimes just the illusion. This type of jump eventually fell out of favour. Detractors of these 'flying' fences, however, forget that pure Show Jumpers drop considerably from the greater heights they have cleared in ascendance.

To some extent Badminton had scared off much international competition and Weldon's rider frightener courses certainly encouraged the 'who dares wins' mentality. The era also saw an upturn in Britain's Olympic fortunes.

They won team gold and individual silver in Mexico 1968 and team and individual gold at Munich in 1972. Ironically this may have led Weldon to his only disaster as course builder in 1973, when a third of the field never got beyond fence three.

Frank Weldon's style was splendidly autocratic, and he was not beyond rejecting entries from perfectly qualified competitors if he didn't think they were up to his challenge. As he wrote in one of his Event previews, 'Admirable though it may be for any competitor to have a burning ambition to ride at Badminton, it is downright reprehensible to risk hurting a horse to achieve it, if he or his rider are not ready.' The legal people would probably call it restriction of trade today, but then Weldon's word was law.

It was in his seventy-fifth year that he decided to stand down, having presided over the date change from April to May in 1988.

In some way reflecting how the sport had progressed from its military origins, Hugh Thomas became the first civilian Director of Badminton. A former Olympic rider and individual bronze medallist at the Burghley World Championships, Hugh had also been second at Badminton in 1976 with Playamar.

In 1988 he had been responsible for designing the Olympic Cross Country course at Seoul, having cut his teeth at Windsor and the Junior and Young Rider European Championships at Rotherfield Park in 1985 and 1986. He had been working for Raymond Brooks–Ward at British Equestrian Promotions in London, and living in Hampshire.

Badminton was, and still is to a certain extent, an outer orbit of the Beaufort Hunt, with the great majority of the Event's team coming from a Gloucestershire background. To this end Hugh might have been considered a bit of an outsider, but his qualification for the job was such that it didn't take him long to make his own mark.

Sensibly he didn't change everything straight away, because Weldon's legacy was the greatest Event of its type in the world. Whitbread remained as sponsors only for another three years, so it was fortunate that Hugh's job at BEP was as a sponsorship consultant. He negotiated the deal with the Cirencester-based Colt Car Company, and The Mitsubishi Motors Badminton Horse Trials were presented in 1992.

Weldon's was a hard act to follow, but the sport was changing considerably. Modern sensitivities wouldn't accommodate the attrition rates produced by the 'old and bold' courses. The emphasis was moving further towards more technical skill than just out and out bravado. The Endurance phase was becoming less important and the international rules made this part shorter and shorter until they disappeared completely in 2006. There was also pressure from the International Olympic Committee to make the sport more inclusive to ensure its place in the Games.

There is no doubt that courses which had more finishers attracted more international entries. Recently the Event has had entries from as many as 14 nations. Hugh also has undertaken extensive groundwork to make the going on the track and arena consistent, and he instigated the popular placing of the start and finish of the Cross Country in the main ring.

No sooner has one Event finished, than thoughts for the next one come to mind. There are debriefs from each department and the de-rigging of the enormous infrastructure. Hugh will then start thinking of his new course in the autumn, when any heavy earth moving

will need to be done.

Jane Tuckwell, the Assistant Director, was recruited by Frank Weldon in the Beaufort hunting field, where her father, Major Gerald Gundry, was a joint Master. She came to help in the Badminton office in 1974 and like so many involved with the Trials, Jane has been an integral and dedicated part of the organisation for a long time. (Indeed one of the Director's tact challenges is how to persuade some volunteers, who have served for a very long time, that it might be the moment to hang up the Bowler hat).

While Hugh is in charge, Jane is the office power house and has her finger on the pulse of some of the more mundane

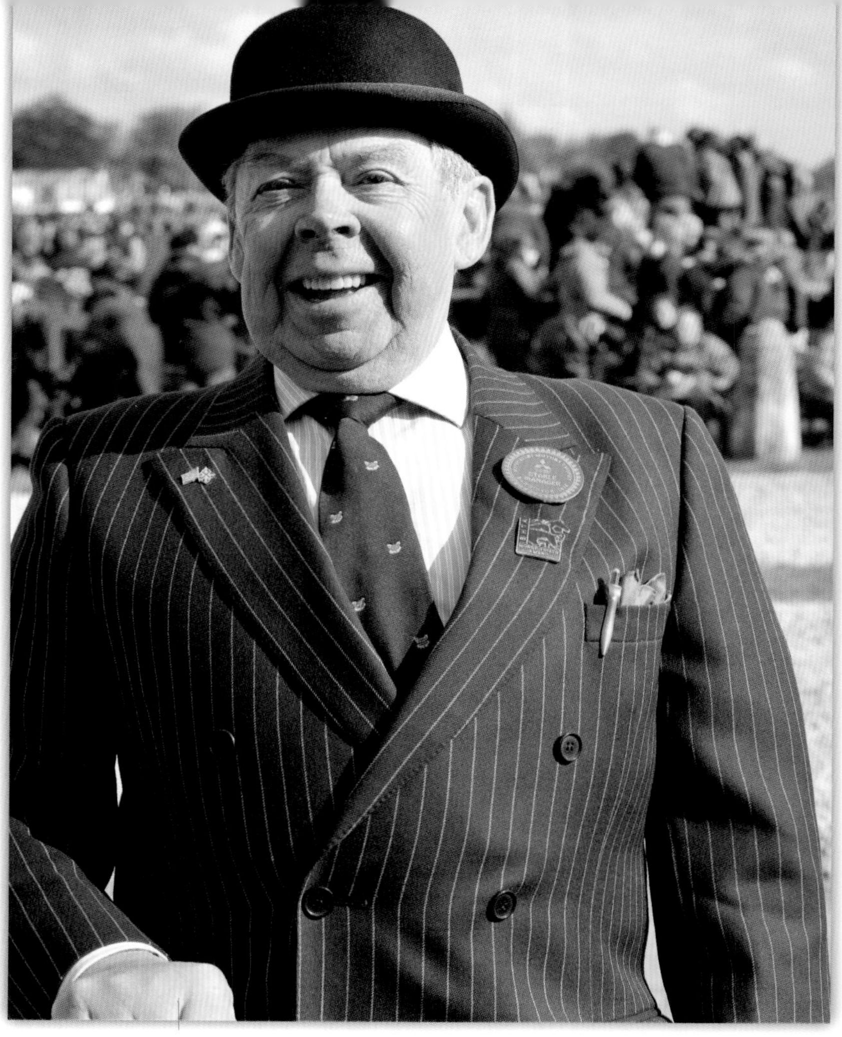

Right: *Former Stud Groom Brian Higham*

details. Two major subjects that exercise her after entries are the trade stands, which have now grown to accommodate over 500 outlets and putting together the programme for the spectators to buy during the Event.

Despite working for Badminton full time Jane also runs a smaller Horse Trials at her home at Shipton Moyne.

Jane's assistant, Sue Ansell, has also worked in the office for over 20 years and is the one for whom the technological revolution of recent times holds no fears. She had been the main link with the Event's website contractor and also helped create the Badminton phone app.

Sue's sister, Vicky Iddon, recently moved up to running the box office, which by definition is not a full time post, but an absolute hive of activity from January until the Event, helped by three assistants.

Some time ago Willa Harford helped in the office, then left to raise her family, when Sue arrived. As Sue took on more responsibility Willa's spot was then taken for several years by one-off interns (every other one seemingly called Holly), until Willa returned. She now is the first voice one hears on ringing the Event and also handles invoices.

There are now so many passes and pieces of paperwork to send that Pam Twissel is now on board, ensconced in Badminton's old post office, surrounded by boxes of mailing.

Harry Verney is a gentleman forester, or as his daughter described him in a national newspaper, a lumberjack. He is also the site manager for Badminton, looking after logistics, facilities/water/electricity/health and safety, and works closely with all the contractors. He performs the same task at other large outdoor events.

Jim Gilmore, who sadly died in 2012, retired as Press Officer after over 30 years in the post, and your author took over in 2002. Though the job is based mainly in London, it is nevertheless a year-round commitment, again picking up fast in the January. A large press corps has to be accredited and passes sent out.

Essential to a horse trial is its Cross Country course, and someone has to possess the skills to realise the designer's concept. In the early years of Badminton it was the estate workers who did the building, but the construction became more sophisticated, and substantial earthworks were required. Alan Willis and his three brothers, Ken, Brian and Gerald, who were originally contracted in the Sixties to build crowd barriers, were drafted in to help with jump construction under George Stoneham. Fifty years on it is Alan and his sons, James and Timmy, who head the team, and their Badminton expertise has led them to building jobs at the Barcelona Olympics and sole responsibility for both the courses that were required for the Sydney Games.

The Willis Bros have been perfect to interpret the ideas of Weldon and Thomas, both insisting their courses have empathy with their surroundings, with the minimum of superfluous adornment. This is a challenge today as many jumps are not built in situ, but at Willis HQ and sited round the park. Portable jumps are economical and versatile; indeed several obstacles from the Olympic course at Greenwich (not a Willis oeuvre) have been making guest appearances at the top events, including Badminton.

The Willis Bros team are also responsible for helping to develop a special frangible (breakable) pin which allows a solid fence to collapse if hit very hard. These have already prevented several serious accidents.

All changes during the Trials when the number of people on site explodes. First there is the army of people involved with the competition side of things.

There are three members of the Ground Jury, the top officials who are in charge of proceedings. They will, with veterinary advice, oversee the horse inspections. Their most high profile task is to judge the Dressage tests. The Technical Delegate, a living rule book and Federation expert, will guide and advise the Ground Jury.

There is a team of vets and doctors; human and horse ambulances; an air ambulance; the stable manager, Margaret Hopkins, who is the Badminton Stud Groom and her team; ring stewards; Cross Country jump judges; a time-keeping team; mounted members of local Pony Clubs who collect the score sheets from the jump judges; an arena party for the Jumping phase, a team at Cross Country control who monitor any of the three horses on the course at any time; radio operators reporting to 'control'; a roster of public address commentators; course crossing stewards; Media Centre assistants and anti-doping monitors.

Quite apart from the equestrian side, an event the size of Badminton has hundreds of people in other roles. There are those concerned with traffic, crowd control, catering, shops, signage, security and most importantly temporary lavatories for about 150,000 people. Much of this is done by outside organisations and contractors.

The TV professionals have their own compound with an entire crew of technicians, camera crew, producers, directors, commentators and presenters. They will also make use of the facilities in the Media Centre, deciding on the 'colour' pieces to shoot and who they might want to interview.

The Horse Trials Office's permanent site is in a single storey building in Badminton High Street opposite the village shop, but decamps into the park during the Trials. The front desk fields requests from the public, while behind a screen an extended admin team deals with everything from official vehicle distribution, special passes, endless phone calls from the public and the general smooth running and inevitable troubleshooting during the extended week.

Spectators

As noted at the start, the very first Badminton in 1949 attracted a surprisingly healthy crowd of 6,000, which went up to 19,000 in year two and 55,000 by 1951. It has settled for many years at about 150,000 over the four days of competition, taking into account that a substantial number come on all days. Obviously the Cross Country day is the biggest draw, as there is space for a large crowd and, though bad weather can put off the last–minute visitor, many fans come regardless. Gates are about 100,000, making Badminton one of the biggest one-day sporting crowd pullers in the world.

Of course one of Badminton's draws is the beautiful parkland over which the course is run, and by definition it is in the depths of the countryside. Though the estate is not far from junctions 17 and 18 of the M4 Motorway, and off the major A46, the approaches are all down narrow country lanes. Over the years, in conjunction with the police, traffic plans have been devised for Cross Country day. Visitors are advised to leave lots of time to make sure they arrive before the action starts at around midday. Patience is the virtue, as it has been known to take an hour from the motorway to the parking spot. Clever back routes and reliance on satnavs are pointless, as a polite policeman will redirect a miscreant and add to the journey time.

While sitting in the inevitable queue,

however, visitors can tune into the dedicated Radio Badminton station, whose wavelength is posted on traffic signs. There will be traffic updates, interviews, discussions and features.

On arrival it is worth first-time visitors identifying a landmark, so that after a long day's spectating they have some idea where they have parked the car. The Badminton crowd is very varied and unlike an event such as Royal Ascot, there is no dress code. Of course there will be many examples of green-wellied, maroon-trousered, tweed-capped and jacketed followers, but an equal amount of people are in jeans, sweatshirts, and fleece jackets. Indeed in recent years the choices of appropriate country wear has grown enormously. The only recommendation is comfort and warmth. High heels and floaty dresses are not a good idea.

There are many ways of getting a ticket for Badminton. The box office opens in early January and there are all sorts of packages to be had. There is a single price for a car on all days and a sliding price for occupants, depending on the day (Cross Country being the top price). There is a considerable reduction for a season ticket. Tickets can be bought

The British Horse Society

BADMINTON
3 DAYS EVENT

APRIL 20th, 21st and 22nd
1949

PROGRAMME

TWO SHILLINGS AND SIXPENCE.

at the several entrances, which are a bit more expensive than pre-booked. On receipt of advance tickets, customers will be sent more detailed travel information.

For many years groups such as Riding Clubs and Pony Clubs have chartered coaches to come to Badminton, which all park over the road from the main event area and next to the air strip, where a dozen or so jetsetter visitors whizz in.

For those who want to really get into the festival spirit, there is a caravan park in easy walking distance from the action (and the village shop), which now has over 1,000 slots. The Glastonbury tendency sleep in tents, and others bring their horse boxes. Running water and ample loos are on hand.

Otherwise there are lots of other forms of accommodation close to Badminton, which can be accessed via the website www.badminton-horse. co.uk . There are five-star hotels aplenty in the Cotswolds and historic towns such as Tetbury and Bath are nearby. There are budget hotels near Bristol, pubs and

bed and breakfasts all around. Places to stay often get booked year on year and many landlords insist on a season booking. Some may indeed bump up their prices for their once a year bonanza. When the Event had to be cancelled in 2012 one report suggested that the local economy had been hit by 50 million pounds. Badminton is big business.

On entering the showground there are kiosks selling A5 pocket-sized programmes, which contain running orders, mini biographies of the contestants, lists of the officials, illustrations of all the Cross Country jumps – painted for over 40 years by Caroline Bromley-Gardner – a map of the course, a map and listing of the trade stands and glossy advertisements.

Apart from a small number of prime seats, viewing the Dressage is free, but for a small price spectators can buy small radio headsets and listen to an expert Dressage commentary. During the tests there is no PA address, as it would distract the horses.

Above: *The Badminton Shop*

On the Dressage days the Cross Country course is open for all to walk round, though no longer with the chance to walk right up to the jumps, as the turf must be protected. It is very likely that riders will be spotted doing one of their three or four walks round the track, working out, to the inch, their routes at the obstacles.

There are lots of features to help make a visit to Badminton a great family day out. For those for whom walking is a difficulty, mobility scooters are available.

For shopaholics there is a drop off area for purchases, for careless parents there is a lost children's pound, and for bored children, the fairground.

If the weather is good, nothing could be better than a picnic at the back of the family car before setting off to take in the action. There are also lots of food choices to be found on sale. There is a big screen at the hub of the showground with a surrounding fast food area selling hog roast, toasted sandwiches and sweets. There is also a tented pub. Elsewhere

there is more up market fare in a wine bar environment.

Badminton has its own merchandising stand with specialist designer shirts, jackets, scarves and gifts. Badminton can almost run to the old boast of a well known Knightsbridge store that claimed you could buy anything there. The variety covers the obvious country clothing stands to rural crafts, which offer garden furniture, designer silks and knickknacks, through to a whole food marquee, where all sorts of kitchen implements and sauces are for sale.

There have been Bond Street jewellery stores, estate agents, joke shops, a chemist and a car showroom presenting the sponsor's latest models. In recent years there has also been a bookmaker. To make all this easier there are also cash points. Like so much of Badminton, there is long-time loyalty with the trade stands, some of whom have been there for up to 50 years.

There are many ways to enjoy the Cross Country day. The sedentary

Above: *The big screen*

option is to plonk down by the big screen, having dropped off the shopping, and watch every rider, with just a short amble to the pub or burger stall.

The slightly more adventurous will have got lunch out of the way and amble to one or two jumps quite close to the centre of proceedings, then find a spot by the Lake, which is conveniently close, and enjoy the action with the house as a backdrop.

Real aficionados will gather up their dogs and children and see a couple of competitors start in the main arena then set off round the course in order, seeing at least one combination over each jump. With 80 starters they might, at a push, be able to see a couple at each fence, and end up back at base at the end of the day. Despite the large crowd at each obstacle, visibility is good as the fences now tend to be in clusters, and at the more

spectacular ones there are unreserved portable grandstands.

As mentioned before, there are two horse inspections in front of Badminton House, one the evening before the first Dressage day and the final one on the Show Jumping morning. These are open to the public and have become a popular spectator attraction. The trot ups have now become something of a fashion parade for the riders who lead up their horses.

Badminton is now a firmly penned-in date for thousands of annual pilgrims. There are people who have been going every time for over 50 years and those three generations on; parents who bring their children and groups of young adults who arrange to meet up at specified times; young girls who have come to see their heroines like Mary King and Pippa Funnell, and those welcome visitors for whom it is their first visit.

LITTLE BOOK OF **BADMINTON**

End Piece

Badminton might have been accused of over selling itself back in 1949 when it called itself The Greatest Horse Event in Great Britain, but the title was surprisingly prescient. Through the foresight and generosity of the 10th Duke of Beaufort; the encouragement and secretarial input from the British Horse Society; the planning and course design skills of Trevor Horn, for whom the whole venture was a leap in the dark; the boldness of a group of civilian riders, including ladies, who joined the soldiers in this military sport, and the 6,000 members of the public who turned out to support the venture, who by word of mouth set in motion a surge of interest, one of the world's greatest annual sporting events, that far transcends both its heritage and equestrian interest, was created.

Badminton can now claim to be The Greatest Horse Event in the World.

Acknowledgements

Published sources for *Little Book of Badminton* include: *Badminton: A Record of the Three Day Event from 1949 to 1969* by Barbara Cooper; *Badminton Horse Trials: The Triumphs And The Tears*, by Debbie Sly; *International Three Day Event, Results and Records from 1912* by Rhydain Wynn-Williams; *Badminton, The Duke of Beaufort and his House* by John Harris; The archives of *Horse & Hound* and *Eventing* magazines. Contemporary photographs are by Kit Houghton; historic photographs, maps and illustrations from Badminton; painting reproductions by courtesy of His Grace the Duke of Beaufort.

The pictures in this book were provided courtesy of the following:

KIT HOUGHTON
WWW.HOUGHTONSHORSES.COM/

Design and artwork by Scott Giarnese

Published by G2 Entertainment Limited

Publishers Jules Gammond and Edward Adams

Written by Julian Seaman

Julian Seaman has been Media Officer at Badminton since 2002. He rode at the Event in the late Seventies and has contributed to many equestrian magazines. He published a personal account of the Trials, *Badminton Revisited, An Anecdotal History* (JR Books 2009).